on track ...
The Smashing Pumpkins

1991-2000

every album, every song

Matt Karpe

sonicbondpublishing.com

Sonicbond Publishing Limited
www.sonicbondpublishing.co.uk
Email: info@sonicbondpublishing.co.uk

First Published in the United Kingdom 2023
First Published in the United States 2023

British Library Cataloguing in Publication Data:
A Catalogue record for this book is available from the British Library

Copyright Matt Karpe 2023

ISBN 978-1-78952-291-4

Typeset in ITC Garamond Std & ITC Avant Garde Gothic
Printed and bound in England

Graphic design and typesetting: Full Moon Media

Follow us on social media:
Twitter: https://twitter.com/SonicbondP
Instagram: www.instagram.com/sonicbondpublishing_/
Facebook: www.facebook.com/SonicbondPublishing/

Linktree QR code:

on track ...
The Smashing Pumpkins
1991-2000

every album, every song

Matt Karpe

sonicbondpublishing.com

For Carly, always.

on track ...
The Smashing Pumpkins

Contents

In the Beginning

During their original incarnation, The Smashing Pumpkins pushed the boundaries of alternative rock in a way that very few others did. Refusing to stick to one specific sound or subgenre, the band preserved their artistic integrity by doing things on their own terms, and in the process earned a healthy respect from many of their peers. Over the course of the 1990s, the Pumpkins sold well in excess of fifteen million records, they were one of America's most commercially successful bands, and they won multiple awards including two prestigious GRAMMYs. Much of this was down to one man's vision – reinforced by songwriting talent where attention to detail was key.

In the early half of the '80s, William Patrick Corgan Jr. (or Billy as he preferred to be known) was moving away from the Black Sabbath's, Queen's and Van Halen's of the world, having discovered the flourishing new wave and alt rock scenes. Leaning towards the gothic side and with Bauhaus and The Cure in mind, Corgan formed his first band – Coat of Eyes, with three like-minded friends.

A native of Chicago, whose contribution to music history predominantly lay in the scope of blues and jazz (Muddy Waters, Herbie Hancock, Ramsey Lewis etc.), Corgan felt the Windy City would neither appreciate or accept the kind of music his band was trying to create, and in 1985 Coat of Eyes relocated to St. Petersburg, Florida with three of the four original members. Renaming themselves The Marked – the new moniker chosen because of Corgan and drummer Ron Roesing's distinctive port-wine stain birthmarks (Corgan's is on his left arm and on both sides of his hand), the band attempted to build some hype through playing live shows in the area. Early recordings of some of their songs are still available online, 'Now That I Feel' and 'Ring of Shadow' in particular oozing 1980s vibrancy with jangling guitars and swishing waves of synth – much akin to The Cure's *The Top* and *The Head on the Door* eras. When another member decided to cut his losses, however, Corgan was forced to return to Chicago, where ultimately, The Marked disbanded.

A new venture in Deep Blue Dream followed for Corgan, the stint noteworthy for the involvement of the late Wayne Static. For people familiar with the then-known Wayne Wells' industrial metal outfit from the late 1990s, Static-X, hearing Deep Blue Dream songs such as 'Goals' and 'Into My Hands' reveal an incredible difference in the vocalist's delivery, his later harsh and visceral styles nowhere in sight on dreamy new wave anthems powered along by Simon Le Bon or Martin Gore-esque pitch and range.

In 1988, Deep Blue Dream recorded an EP through Chicago's Criterion Records, but Corgan was not present for the studio sessions because he was already putting the wheels in motion for another project. Not long after the EP's release, Corgan moved on and Deep Blue Dream eventually called it quits. Wells moved to Los Angeles and formed Static-X in 1994, when at the same time, he adopted his more famous stage name. On the back of the release of the debut album *Wisconsin Death Trip* in 1999, Static-X became a platinum-selling band and one of the frontrunners of the expansive nu metal movement.

Now working in a local record store, Corgan would tell colleagues and customers he was in a band called The Smashing Pumpkins, an instantly memorable name already lodged in his brain long before anything would come to fruition with it. While working a shift at the record store, Corgan met James Iha for the first time – a second-generation Japanese American who was majoring in graphic design at the city's Loyola University. He also happened to be a rather talented guitar player.

The two young men hit it off straight away and when they decided to start a band together, The Smashing Pumpkins was born. Corgan moved to the bass guitar as well as assuming the lead vocal role, while a drum machine was utilised to get some early songs off the ground. Before the end of 1988, the duo had already recorded and released their first demo tape, titled *Nothing Ever Changes*. Heavily influenced by The Cure and New Order, and also containing elements of Echo & the Bunnymen and Fields of the Nephilim, the early showcasing of Corgan's songwriting skills was enough to suggest The Smashing Pumpkins was onto something rather interesting. Just as impressive was Iha's haunting guitar leads and textures, especially on the atmospheric and moody salvo of 'The Vigil' and 'Nothing and Everything'. By now, Iha had already dropped out of university to focus on the band full-time, and even on such a raw first offering the four tracks that made up the demo remain captivating listening today. For the two previously mentioned numbers, Corgan brought in his fellow Marked brother Ron Roesing to play the drums, but for the latter 'Holiday' and 'Cross', a drum machine was used instead.

The next addition to the band was D'arcy Wretzky, a self-taught bassist who had not long moved to Chicago from South Haven, Michigan. A lover of post-punk music, she had previously taken a huge leap of faith by eloping to France to join a band, but by the time she had landed in Europe, the band had already called it a day. They say some things are meant to be, and Wretzky's chance meeting with Billy Corgan came after a Dan Reed Network concert. Overhearing Corgan criticising the show he had just witnessed, Wretzky jumped in and became embroiled in a lengthy discussion, which somehow ended up in her being offered the bass gig in The Smashing Pumpkins. With the new addition to the line-up, it allowed Corgan to return to his preferred guitar position and forge a formidable tag team with Iha.

The Pumpkins had already played a number of shows around Chicago and were building a small buzz, but one esteemed venue continued to elude them. Longing to add their name to a long list of up-and-coming acts to have played the Cabaret Metro, who at first welcomed local bands before booking out-of-towners such as R.E.M., Sonic Youth and Metallica, the venue's owner, Joe Shanahan, agreed to book the Pumpkins so long as they ditched their drum machine and hire a real drummer.

Jimmy Chamberlin had been playing the drums since he was nine years old, primarily focusing on jazz but also becoming skilled in Big Band and Latin techniques. Playing in a host of bands around Illinois in his late teens, the last of which he found tough to maintain with their hefty touring schedule, Chamberlin decided to leave music behind and become a carpenter. Meeting Billy Corgan through a mutual contact would lead him to re-evaluate his career path once again, though. Knowing The Smashing Pumpkins were on the hunt for the final piece of their puzzle, Chamberlin reminisced during a later interview on watching the band perform for the first time:

I went out and saw the band – Billy, James, and D'arcy – playing at Avalon with a drum machine. Man, did they sound horrible. They were atrocious. But the thing I noticed was that not only were the song structures good, but Billy's voice had a lot of drive to it, like he was dying to succeed.

Ironically, Corgan had his reservations about Chamberlin too, even before he had heard the drummer play. It was Chamberlin's appearance, the car he drove, and his yellow kit that were a turn-off. However, Jimmy's playing won the frontman over, as Corgan discussed in the same later interview:

We were sort of looking at each other in the eye, thinking, 'This ain't gonna happen; this is not the guy.' But he'd learned all our songs, as only Jimmy can, off the top of his head, and within one practice, we were ready to play. It was amazing. We just knew right away. He's that good.

Chamberlin immediately brought a more intense sound to the Pumpkins, which in turn moved the band away from the style of the *Nothing Ever Changes* demo towards diverse and multi-layered songs led by distorted guitars and lyrics full of Corgan's poetic angst.

Funnily enough, there was a scene coming up in Seattle at the same time which appeared to perfectly encompass what the Chicago foursome were doing, although the Pumpkins were less inspired by the underground punk and rock acts as many of their West Coast contemporaries seemed to be.

On 5 October 1988, the Metro hosted the Pumpkins for the first time, and in the following year, the band released two more demos – *The Smashing Pumpkins* and *Moon*. Both tapes solidified the line-up as a collective force even though Corgan was the main songwriter and overall leader, but perhaps more importantly, at the time, it helped them adjust to being in recording studios and working with outside producers and engineers. Also in 1989, the quartet made their first recorded appearance when they were included on the Halo Records compilation album, *Light into Dark*, which was dedicated to promoting Chicago-based rock bands. 'Sun' and 'My Dahlia' were featured on the CD and vinyl release – the former being a track originally written by Corgan for The Marked.

The Smashing Pumpkins were ready for full lift-off. Each member was dedicated to the cause, but it was Billy Corgan's drive which was set to spearhead the band into a new decade, where the music industry was ready to say goodbye to the hair metal wave and welcome in a new era of heavier guitar-orientated songs which were just as capable of earning some strong mainstream appeal.

*This book contains the songs officially released between 1990-2000. It does not include those later unveiled on the 2011, 2012, 2013 and 2014 album reissues.

Single Release – 'I Am One' (Corgan, Iha)
Recorded at Reel Time Studios towards the end of 1989 with the college tuition funds left for Corgan by his late grandmother, The Smashing Pumpkins released their first official single in May 1990 through the independent label Limited Potential.

Just 1500 copies of 'I Am One' were pressed – a song ideal for the Pumpkins to announce themselves to a wider audience than they had been able to thus far. With enough input from James Iha to earn him a rare co-writing credit, this accessible but energetic alt-rocker was built around the opening drum riff and chugging bass lead. From the moment Corgan and Iha's guitars build into a theatrical onslaught of raw power, the Pumpkins turn from young pretenders to future superstars; the united front put on by all four members showing a combined talent far beyond their lean years.

The theme surrounding 'I Am One' is religion, its lyrical content devised by Corgan after approaching the subject during an LSD trip. Referencing the father, sun, and holy ghost in the song's very first line – 'I am one as you are three, try to find messiah in your trinity' – Corgan initially feared 'I Am One' may cast him as somewhat of an egomaniac when in fact, his intention was to help others look at themselves as they considered in which direction they wanted their lives to go.

With the addition of a double-guitar solo, something the band would incorporate in further songs as their career progressed, The Smashing Pumpkins had set their stall out in grand fashion with a confidence, swagger, and total belief in the art they were creating.

'Not Worth Asking' (Corgan)
Chosen as the B-side for the 'I Am One' single, 'Not Worth Asking' is a lighter track than its predecessor, but it does offer an early insight into the Pumpkins' knack of creating a quiet/loud dynamic in their songs, which they would become known for later in the decade.

An angst-fuelled song where Corgan appears to be reminiscing about a lost love ('I'm on my own, not worth being, I might already be, I just want someone to reach for me'), an innocence to the songwriter quickly draws in the listener through a tender vocal over a punchy rhythm section where D'arcy Wretzky's bass is higher up the mix. As the second chorus arrives, so do some heavier bouts of guitar, both bold and meaty and fitting of the rising tension the song produces across its four-minute-plus running time.

'Not Worth Asking' is a popular B-side that many a fan has mentioned amongst their favourite Pumpkins songs, and the quartet would amass an incredible amount of material throughout the 1990s, which would end up being relegated to the unreleased and rarities pile, when they could easily have been included on the albums they were written for.

Single Release – 'Tristessa' (Corgan)

The Pumpkins' second single of 1990 proved to be their one and only output on Sub Pop – the independent label formed by Bruce Pavitt and Jonathan Poneman, which would achieve considerable success by helping grunge's ascension on the back of having Nirvana, Soundgarden and Mudhoney on their roster.

The song's title is taken from the Jack Kerouac novel of the same name – the Tristessa in this instance, being a Mexican prostitute, and Billy Corgan creates a grinding rock track where his gravelly vocal tones are punctuated with some tender melodies, a young and fresh singer possessing confidence in abundance as he declares his love through passages of sensitive lyricism.

Released in the December and promoted by Sub Pop as their single of the month, 'Tristessa' features riffs aplenty and a joyous accent of Jimmy Chamberlin's drum sections. Unlike most of the acts who were happy to be on Sub Pop's books, The Smashing Pumpkins were never going to hang around for too long, and despite Corgan revealing years later how he regretted releasing 'Tristessa' as a single, the song joined 'I Am One' in helping attract significant interest from a handful of major record labels.

For the single's cover art, Corgan and Iha flank a focal-pointed D'arcy, while Chamberlin is relegated to occupying the rear cover because he failed to show up for the original photo shoot.

'La Dolly Vita' (Corgan)

The B-side to 'Tristessa' on the US 7" vinyl, 'La Dolly Vita' takes its name from the 1960 satirical comedy *La Dolce Vita* (meaning 'The Sweet Life'), the Pumpkins' take having stemmed from an inside joke between the band members.

Recorded on the same day as the release's lead song, this mid-paced and rather sombre number glides along with more heartfelt poetry from Corgan ('La dolly vita, sweet as true love, la dolly vita, cool as ice cream). Later included on the *Pisces Iscariot* rarities album in 1994, Corgan wrote in its liner notes of the personal memories relating to 'La Dolly Vita', signing off with the poignant admittance of 'Be careful what you say, but be careful what you don't say'.

During its 4:20 length, the Pumpkins decided to ramp up the volume in its final third, where Chamberlin shines on a blistering drum solo, as Iha and Corgan replace subtle guitar effects with a short but sharp burst of heavy distortion.

'Honeyspider' (Corgan)

Germany received a special 12" vinyl release of 'Tristessa' and they were also given a bonus track in the form of 'Honeyspider', which first appeared on the 1989 *Moon* demo tape. Dreamy and with gothic nuances, the lack of a chorus is not an issue because the song's charm comes from the hypnotising guitars and tentative drum fills.

With this vinyl pressing, first-time listeners of the band were treated to three sonically disparate tracks, but all of them are equally intriguing in their own way.

Gish (1991)

Personnel:
Billy Corgan: lead vocals, guitar, bass
James Iha: guitar, backing vocals
D'arcy Wretzky: bass, backing vocals
Jimmy Chamberlin: drums
Recorded at: Smart Studios, Madison, Wisconsin (December 1990-March 1991)
Produced by: Butch Vig, Billy Corgan
Record label: Caroline
Release date: 28 May 1991
Chart positions: US: 195, NZ: 40
Running time: 45:45

In a weird kind of way, *Gish* is almost like an instrumental album – it just happens to have singing on it, but the music overpowers the band in a lot of places. I was trying to say a lot of things I couldn't really say in kind of intangible, unspeakable ways, so I was capable of doing that with the music, but I don't think I was capable of doing it with words.
Billy Corgan.

Receiving multiple major label offers by December 1990, the Pumpkins elected to sign to Caroline Records – an independent label based in New York whose pitch appeared all the more appealing due to their affiliation with the high-rolling Virgin Records. Before the year was out, the quartet were already holed up in a studio working on their debut album, with a $20,000 budget and the relatively unknown producer Butch Vig in tow.

Before the Pumpkins came calling, Vig had been more at home working with bands who had little to no budget, and whose studio time was kept to the bare minimum to avoid running up costs. Repeatedly collaborating with noise rockers Killdozer throughout the 1980s, Vig also produced the US alternative crew Urge Overkill, Laughing Hyenas, and The Fluid in the run-up to first meeting The Smashing Pumpkins, but Billy Corgan's entourage were a different breed entirely.

Recorded in 30 days at Vig's Smart Studios in Madison, Wisconsin, Corgan wrote almost all of the songs and performed much of the guitar and bass parts, much to the chagrin of his fellow band members. Corgan's search of perfection could easily have cost his band's career before it had truly begun but somehow, they were able to make it out the other side – just. Vig and Corgan's personalities may have clashed at first, but the two were able to push each other creatively, intently focusing on various tones and textures, which would ultimately give *Gish* its effervescent complexity. The incomparable sound of Jimmy Chamberlin's drums was also made possible by Vig – a drummer himself, who understood how every facet had to be covered to give the album every chance of standing out in an over-saturated alternative rock crowd.

15

A box of lavish delights, *Gish* is at times sonically visceral and dark, but in equal parts psychedelic and introspective. The amalgam of heavy rockers and shimmering ballads may have stemmed from Corgan's vast and eclectic influences, but to be able to competently fuse so many elements into a band's debut record, and filling it with limitless depth and density, was virtually unheard of in the indie scene circa 1991.

'An album of spiritual ascension' was how Corgan described *Gish* in a 1995 interview with *MTV*, and upon its 28 May release in 1991, the Pumpkins' first official full-length offering was met with an overly positive response. The styles covered across the ten tracks were always going to be a major selling point, and *Gish* particularly caught the attention and imagination of teenagers across America – so much so that it reached number one on the College Music Journal (*CMJ*) chart which tracked airplay on college radio stations throughout the country.

Managing one week on the *Billboard* 200 by creeping in at 195, *Gish* also reached six on the Heatseekers Chart – recently launched as a way to highlight sales by up-and-coming artists. Over in New Zealand, a six-week stint on the national album listings led to a peak position of 40. In its first year, *Gish* sold a respectable 100,000 copies and became the biggest-selling independent album of all time. That record remained intact until Orange County punks The Offspring claimed the throne in 1994 upon the release of their third album, *Smash*.

Gish was certified gold in the US on 14 March 1994, and five years later, it finally reached platinum status by hitting the one million sales mark. Butch Vig's stock would also rise on the back of working with the Pumpkins, and within a matter of weeks of finishing *Gish*, he was back in the studio with Nirvana and producing their legendary sophomore record, *Nevermind*. It only went on to sell 30 million copies worldwide. 'Only'.

'I Am One' (Corgan, Iha)
Re-recorded for inclusion on *Gish* but a facsimile of the version distributed through Limited Potential, Billy Corgan would later admit his regret at not re-working 'I Am One' in any way. Luckily, the Pumpkins fans didn't seem to mind too much, and the song remains one of the band's best opening tracks from any of their albums.

During an episode of Corgan's *Thirty-Three* podcast in October 2022, he briefly discussed how both LSD and religion played influential roles in the genesis of the song's lyrical content:

'I Am One' was my grappling with the idea that I've been told a bunch of stuff about religion, particularly in the catholic church, that I knew in my heart wasn't true. That Jesus is a saviour wasn't really saying the things they said he was saying; at least, that is my interpretation. LSD, in particular, got me to think beyond what I was told and realise, oh no, we're actually all connected. The song isn't as much about me, as it is trying to figure who I was going to be.

'I Am One' was the second single taken from *Gish*, hitting radio in August 1992. Its best chart performance was 73 in the UK. The music video was directed by Kevin Kerslake, who had already worked on promo clips for Sonic Youth, Soundgarden and Primus. In 1992 alone, Kerslake would direct videos for Pantera ('This Love'), Nirvana ('Come as You Are' and 'Lithium'), and Faith No More ('Midlife Crisis' and 'Everything's Ruined'). His vision for 'I Am One' involved capturing live footage and then using various editing techniques and colour schemes to create an intoxicating spectacle of a typical The Smashing Pumpkins club show in the early 1990s. The shots of Corgan's guitar solos (which incidentally remain his favourite parts of the song) allow a great insight into his playing method, where he seemingly strangles the life out of his guitar to discharge as much emotion as he humanly can. Despite Kerslake's reputation of being a talented director, the Pumpkins were less impressed, and after seeing the final video cut, they decided to shelve it for almost a decade. It was finally released on their *Greatest Hits Video Collection* in 2001.

'Siva' (Corgan)

Pronounced 'Shiva' and in reference to the god considered one of the 'Holy Trinity' within the Hindu religion and known equally as 'The Great God' and 'The God of Destruction', Billy Corgan once considered 'Siva' as a potential name for his band before settling on The Smashing Pumpkins. Instead, Corgan recycled the title and used it for the song he revealed he considers to be the first to truly define the band's sound.

Although released three months after *Gish* came out, 'Siva' is the album's official lead single and fared best in New Zealand's chart, reaching 45. The song's main riff was birthed and demoed on an acoustic guitar during Billy's record store-working days, but once it was re-ignited on an electric guitar, it bred a whole new life of its own. 'That riff sounded like my band – it had instant identity', said Corgan when reminiscing on 'Siva'. 'It got my blood going right away. There was something about it that was so distinctive that it made a lot of other songs I'd written seem wimpy and weak by comparison.'

It is the raw heaviness of the track that many a listener embraced, though. Fusing '80s alternative metal with trappings of psych rock much akin to what Jane's Addiction was coming out with on their *Nothing's Shocking* and *Ritual De Lo Habitual* records, 'Siva' is presented at breakneck speed and with a heavy groove during its first half, even incorporating a guitar solo which stands out through the use of a Big Muff fuzzbox pedal – a piece of equipment the band would more frequently use further down the line. Out of nowhere and creating a nice mood change, two reflective passages precede further raucous jousts of instrumentation, but the fluctuations only enhance a newfound fascination with The Smashing Pumpkins, which many could attest to upon hearing *Gish* for the first time.

When performing 'Siva' live in the early days, Billy would introduce it as 'A song about killing parents and taking drugs', but in later years revealed the lyrics to have served as a 'personal manifesto', the line of 'Way down deep beneath my heart lies a soul that's torn apart, tell me what you're after, I just want to get there faster' alluding to a longing for emotional acceptance.

Calling on a young Angela Conway to direct what at the time was the band's first music video, 'Siva' contains psychedelic and religious connotations via vivid imagery of holy figurines and mystical masks. Each band member is at one point shown submerged in a bath, and the various colour schemes only add to a rich treatment, which makes 'Siva' almost as important visually as it is audibly.

'Rhinoceros' (Corgan)

Switching tempo from what came before, the Pumpkins enter ballad territory for the mesmeric 'Rhinoceros', where Billy writes of a girl and an ice cream party. First recorded in 1989 at Reel Time Studios, the rendition heard by the masses shows just how far the band had come in such a short space of time, thanks in no small part to Butch Vig's efforts in adding a smooth gleam over the record. Using a 24-track console and filling twenty-two of the tracks with instrumentation, this tremolo guitar-led dreamy saga came to be thanks to another Corgan dabble with LSD. 'LSD gave me the confidence to attempt these things of kind of a weird tightrope wire act,' the singer so eloquently put it during a later interview, and the sounds emanating from 'Rhinoceros' certainly give off a hazy and contemplative feel.

Cleaner cut both rhythmically and vocally, this 6:30 rollercoaster of emotions builds to a pulsating crescendo as Jimmy Chamberlin's effortless drum fills formulate around a screeching and now customary guitar solo. Often thrown into the grunge category because of the timeframe in which the Pumpkins earned their big break, 'Rhinoceros' can perhaps be considered the closest the Chicago four-piece came to justifying the sub-genre's tag; even though they were already proving to be so much more than a one-trick pony.

'Bury Me' (Corgan)

Big on riffs but progressive in its delivery, 'Bury Me' returns to the heaviness of the album's opening salvo and features a masterclass in guitar playing from both Corgan and Iha. Overdosing on scathing feedback and containing further solos which continued to bring a newfound respect after their often-maligned additions to the hair metal anthems of the 1980s, it is likely that many a listener would have been inclined to pick up a six-stringed instrument for the first time upon hearing this gem of a song, where multiple tones are adeptly overdubbed atop one another.

Written two years before the *Gish* sessions, 'Bury Me' further excels through D'arcy's deep bass rhythms and Jimmy's rapid drum takes, and with everything combined, is enough to pull the listener one way and then another in spectacular if not disorientating fashion.

'I often forget songs like these exist, but they are a testament to a faith I once had, now forgotten,' wrote Corgan in the ominous liner notes of the *Gish* 2011 reissue. Touching on the ambiguous lyrical content where the opening line of 'Bury me in love, bury me in blood' offered a quick dive into an unforeseen darkness, Corgan deterred ideas of specific focus points by simply writing of the song being 'buried beneath non-meaning'. Regardless, 'Bury Me' remains memorable for being another classic The Smashing Pumpkins guitar anthem.

'Crush' (Corgan)

Shapeshifting back to ballad territory with an acoustic lead and an opulent shoegaze backing, 'Crush' is an ode to Corgan's then-girlfriend and future wife, Christine Fabian; the lyrics written while she lay sleeping next to the frontman. 'And this feeling shivers down your spine, love comes in colours, I can't deny' sings Billy with gentle trepidation in his voice, as a pessimism he cannot quite shake threatens to burst the bubble on his hope of a bright future.

Originally given the title of 'Trippy Hippy', a sauntering bass line and minimal percussion highlights the paradox in which *Gish* has presented itself thus far, but the thankfully renamed 'Crush' confirms that sometimes less is more as this romantic heart-filler provides the ideal soundtrack to sit back, lose yourself in the moment, and join Billy Corgan in a rare celebration of love. The soppy sod.

'Suffer' (Corgan)

Following 'Crush' and musically remaining in a pensive mood, 'Suffer' is the most inventive song on the album due to its unusual structure (played in a 3/4 time signature), and distinctive guitar tones.

Once again shrouded in psychedelic servitude, The Smashing Pumpkins show they aren't just about raw power as the slow and slithering 'Suffer' revels in its Doors-esque precision as if born straight out of the sixties. Using jazz as a primary influence when learning to play the drums, Chamberlin is able to show off what he was taught over Wretzky's bluesy bass riff and light atmospheric guitar flourishes. In some ways, 'Suffer' comes off as an extended mid-album interlude, allowing both the band and the audiophile to draw breath and take stock of what has come so far.

'To ascend from the wounds of desire and pain, you must rise from the mounds of desire and change,' sings a shrewd Corgan, on a track that poetically details the trials and tribulations of growing up. An unheralded high point of *Gish*.

'Snail' (Corgan)

An early favourite of Corgan's, 'Snail' is another outing which, like 'Crush', offers a hint of optimism, the lyrics providing a sense of encouragement in chasing your dreams. Hitting the five-minute mark but never at all feeling overlong because of everything that is happening, 'Snail' is a fine example of how the Pumpkins were able to fuse lush melodies with heaviness and distortion – something which, from the off would separate them from their grunge contemporaries.

From the low-key intro, which then erupts into a plethora of fuzzy guitars and simplistic but organic bass grooves, this poignant opus is just what people were looking to acclimatise themselves with during the '90s alternative rock boom, the volume consistently rising and receding to great effect.

'It's a song that wasn't one of those that when you play it, you say, "Hey, this is a really great song,"' discussed Corgan during *Gish*'s tenth-anniversary celebrations, before disclosing 'Snail' had to be continually worked on until the whole band had finally reached a point where they were happy with it. The results were surely appreciated by the hardcore following, even if the casual Pumpkins listener may have bypassed 'Snail' in favour of the more popular tracks that came higher up in the tracklisting.

'Tristessa' (Corgan)

As with 'I Am One', 'Tristessa' was re-recorded for inclusion on *Gish*, with the only audible difference compared to the Sub Pop release being eight seconds shorter in length. If it isn't broken, don't fix it is the lesson here because the Jack Kerouac-inspired hard rocker sounds just as good as it did upon its arrival some seventeen months prior. But what can be said is that even eight tracks into *Gish*, 'Tristessa' continues to build momentum and while many a band may have been running on empty at such a stage of their first offering, The Smashing Pumpkins still have plenty left in the tank.

Unlike 'I Am One' though, 'Tristessa' was not considered for a second single release, and it was also surprising that when the band announced their Greatest Hits compilation album in 2001 (*Rotten Apples*), neither of the early independent singles were included amongst the tracklisting. Still an absolute banger three decades later, it is clear why 'Tristessa' alerted major record labels to the Pumpkin's door and were keen on obtaining their signatures.

'Window Paine' (Corgan)

Before Billy Corgan became fully embroiled in the new wave scene, he had been a big fan of British heavy metal icons Black Sabbath, and upon hearing 'Window Paine' for the first time, it was clear there were more than a few hints of the Birmingham mob's masterpiece, 'War Pigs', coming through on this absolute epic.

Steering clear of the doomy overtones created by Ozzy Osbourne and his allies, the Pumpkins instead deliver a dense and lengthy song both experimental and proggy in places, while still sticking with those psychedelic textures which had proved so effective thus far. Appearing to focus on overcoming darkness and feelings of self-pity, a tender-toned Corgan relays over a deep bass chug not too dissimilar to the style of Sabbath's Geezer Butler, while the ambient guitar licks stifle any threat of a metallic breakout. There is clearly a stronger emphasis on instrumentation over lyrical structures; in fact, 'Window Paine' rolls along for over six minutes and reaches a soaring finale courtesy of a blistering Chamberlin drumming display and a sublime if not slightly unsettling rhythm section. A nod to one of Corgan's biggest influences but in no way an imitation, 'Window Paine' is the sign of a young songwriter's true awakening.

'Daydream' (Corgan)

A hazy and acoustic album closer, Corgan confessed to 'Daydream' drawing influence from Irish shoegazers, My Bloody Valentine. The surprise here comes with the vocals, where D'arcy takes the microphone for a soothing and sensual lead. A second version featuring Corgan's vocals was also recorded; however, he later stated D'arcy's voice was 'prettier, more cold, and far away'.

Not quite reaching the two-minute point, there is still time for the inclusion of some cello and violin during its final throes, performed by Mary Gaines and Chris Wagner, respectively, but in truth, 'Daydream' is a rather flat way to close *Gish*, considering the substantial over-indulgence afforded to every track which came ahead of it.

'I'm Going Crazy' (Corgan)

Recorded live in Smart's control room, 'I'm Going Crazy' is a hidden track which begins just a matter of seconds after the conclusion of 'Daydream'.

'I have gone crazy, motherfucking crazy', sings a muffled Corgan, perhaps hinting at the stresses and strains of writing and recording *Gish* almost entirely by himself. At the time, considered nothing more than a joke, this 'song' at least shows the Pumpkins had a lighter and less serious side to them than some may have realised, and thankfully it doesn't discourage from the overall triumph the album turned out to be.

Lull (1991)

Personnel:
Billy Corgan: lead vocals, guitar
James Iha: guitar, backing vocals
D'arcy Wretzky: bass, backing vocals
Jimmy Chamberlin: drums
Recorded at Reel Time Studios, Chicago, Smart Studios, Madison, Wisconsin
(1989-1991)
Produced by: Butch Vig, Billy Corgan
Record label: Caroline
Release date: 5 November 1991
Chart positions: N/A
Running time: 14:17

First released as a promotional single in early 1991, 'Rhinoceros' was given an official issue seven months later when the song was repackaged as an EP with three B-sides. Targeted towards the Pumpkins' already die-hard following, *Lull* was an intriguing title for the short collection even if it has been more commonly known as 'The Rhinoceros Single' during its thirty-plus year existence.

'Rhinoceros' is unsurprisingly the lead track, the only difference from the album version being the cutting of the extended feedback at its close. A music video was filmed to coincide with the EP's release, once again directed by Angela Conway, and split into three main sections. The initial idea for the video was to model it on The Cure's 'Close to Me' clip, where the British goths can be seen confined to a small wardrobe which ends up being thrown over a cliff with the band still inside. The Pumpkins' plan may not have been so agoraphobic or death-defying, but their ode to Robert Smith's entourage was thwarted upon attending the filming location, where they were allocated a much larger room than they desired and with a sound stage to boot. Intentionally spreading themselves apart, when the cameras began rolling, the band members appear bored and disinterested in the day's activities.

The second set of footage stems from a concert at the intimate London Underworld on 6 September 1991; however, the quality of the film wasn't as good as first hoped and so it became relegated to the latter part of the video, tying in with the arrival of Billy Corgan's exquisite guitar solo. Extra footage had to be filmed to avoid the video becoming a farce, so while still in London, the Pumpkins took a handheld video camera into Hyde Park and filmed themselves in various poses and musings. While the final video exercised a mishmash of what was at their disposal at the time, it is all the more wholesome as it showed the band were able to think outside of the box and come up with new ideas when time was of the essence; much like they could do musically when needed.

'Rhinoceros' reached 27 on *Billboard*'s Alternative Airplay chart, and due to its overwhelming popularity, the song has remained a prolific inclusion in the band's setlists up to the present day. And now for the B-sides ...

'Blue' (Corgan)
A potent but melodic hard rocker, 'Blue' continues the quartet's demonstration of the quiet/loud dynamic. With D'arcy's punchy bass and Billy and James' aspiring guitar work, further compensated by Jimmy's rigorous drumming, 'Blue' may be a B-side that lacks a little of the Pumpkins' over-indulgence, but it is a solid track which many a band would love to adopt as one of their finer works.

'Slunk' (Corgan)
An absolute diamond in the rough, 'Slunk' is a scintillating number which rages at breakneck speed and only relents when it reaches its climax. Very much giving off a live feel from the mixing, this is The Smashing Pumpkins with a no holds barred mentality, bereft of experimentation, a simpler but nonetheless memorable song that tends to be forgotten about because of its status of only ever appearing on *Lull* in studio form.

Offering a good example of the chemistry Corgan and Iha had built in such a relatively short time playing together, throw in some supersonic Chamberlin drumming and here you have an angry The Smashing Pumpkins who let loose to create a thoroughly aggressive and breathless hard rock song.

'Bye June' (Corgan)
Recorded in 1989 and debuting on the *Moon* demo, 'Bye June' is a pure acoustic ballad that has long been considered a Billy Corgan solo song. The soulful and innocent vocals highlight a sensitivity the singer possessed as he got to grips with disclosing his emotions on tape, while the lyric 'Bye June, I'm going to the moon, I hope you make it soon' hints at a lost love which continued to strike a raw nerve at the time.

'Bye June' isn't one of the more memorable songs the Pumpkins put their name to, but it is a nice addition to *Lull* which mixes things up and offers a little bit of everything like *Gish* had prior; thus further cementing The Smashing Pumpkins to be alt rock's hottest new band.

Building Momentum

Towards the end of 1991, the Pumpkins joined the Red Hot Chili Peppers as support on a string of US dates to promote the funk rockers' fifth album, *Blood Sugar Sex Magik*. After 1992 had been welcomed in, the quartet jetted off to Europe and then Japan for small club tours and come April, they were playing to their largest crowds yet when opening select arena dates in America for Guns N' Roses, on their *Use Your Illusion* tour. The audiences appeared less receptive to the psychedelic rock on show, though, favouring the sleazy anthems which had turned Axl Rose's clan into global superstars since their debut album, *Appetite for Destruction*, unleashed itself in the summer of 1987.

On 4 April, the monthly music magazine *Reflex* released its latest issue, with hip-hop icon Ice Cube gracing the front cover. As well as featuring an article on the Pumpkins within its contents, the publication's subscribers were also offered a free 7" flexi disc containing 'Daughter' – a track which had first been made available on the *Moon* demo. With a rare co-writing credit for D'arcy Wretzky, this extended version is a bass-driven and mellow affair with gentle vocals and light percussion, and again it offered a shoegaze charm not unlike the work of Jim Morrison and the Doors.

First devised in the early '60s and at that point known as the Eva-tone Soundsheet, the thin and cost-effective flexible vinyl sheets may have had some playability issues with the weight of turntable styluses, but they became increasingly popular when the Beatles began releasing content on them as Christmas treats for their adoring fan club members, in the mid to late part of the decade. Seemingly about a girl that Billy Corgan wants to fall in love with even though he knows he shouldn't ('In the water, just like a snake, someone's daughter, hidden love, slip away'), because of how limited the 'Daughter' flexi was means it remains of the most sought-after pieces of The Smashing Pumpkins musical memorabilia.

On 8 September 1991, the four-piece were invited to London's Maida Vale Studios to record for John Peel's Radio 1 show. A legendary DJ who became best known for promoting up-and-coming artists of all genres, his 'Peel Sessions' often provided the featured guests with their first taste of national coverage, so the Pumpkins visit was a rather big deal even if *Gish* had already earned the band some strong exposure stateside. The UK was a tougher nut to crack, but thanks to their deal with Virgin subsidiary Hut Recordings, who maintained themselves an independent label so they could get their artists onto the UK's Indie Chart, the British market was already accessible for the Pumpkins' early work. Having John Peel fighting your corner was never a bad thing, though.

On the day of recording the *Peel Sessions EP* (officially released on 12" vinyl, CD and cassette on 22 June 1992), the band arrived two hours late due to a miscommunication and were then treated like novices throughout their visit. Corgan later discussed the unsavoury experience:

Recorded for our first BBC session, we were led like lambs to the slaughter by a bored ex-rock star who was assigned to us as session producer (Mott the Hoople founder and drummer, Dale Griffin), and his chief assistant (a cockney who hated our too-loud sound). We were mocked for asking any question, and each and every request to change a sound was met with fake turning of the knobs... The upside from this charade was that in anger we played with ferocious might; one of the few documents we have in studio that captures the way we were meant to destroy music and each other be exalting in its ad infinitum power.

The ferocious might Corgan mentioned is clearly evident on 'Siva', and the *Peel Sessions* recording may just be the best live take of that particular song. The aggressiveness is all down to the stress the band was suffering, as said before, no one has ever been able to bleed emotion through their guitar quite like Billy Corgan. Jimmy Chamberlin sounds just as pissed off, in fact, his unhinged drumming may just eclipse Corgan's playing in this instance.

Next came a meaty cover of the Animals' 'Girl Named Sandoz' – the 'Sandoz' in question referencing the laboratory where LSD was first invented. Released as a B-side on the 'When I Was Young' single in 1967, and the first two songs written by the Eric Burdon/Vic Briggs/John Weider/Barry Jenkins/Danny McCulloch line-up, the Pumpkins' heavier and contemporary rendition is built around stoner-like guitar fuzz and a biting bass groove. Although it wasn't one of the more renowned songs of the Animals' career, it is likely a few people went and checked out the original on the back of hearing the cover, which The Smashing Pumpkins more than made their own. As with 'Siva', 'Girl Named Sandoz' sounds all the better for the added fury which went into the performance, so perhaps the grumpy Dale Griffin can be commended for that, at least.

The usual format of a 'Peel Sessions' show consisted of four tracks being recorded, but for some reason, the Pumpkins only laid down three – the final one being a *Gish* outtake titled 'Smiley'. Slow and melancholic, this one is in stark contrast to the thicker cuts which came before it, but its relatively flat nature indicates why it wasn't deemed good enough to be included on the album it had been written for.

June 1992 was a big month for The Smashing Pumpkins. Around the time of the *Peel Sessions* release, the band signed with Virgin Records. After the major label had been acquired by Thorn EMI, Caroline and many of their artists were merged into Virgin. Thorn's purchase cost them a reported $1 billion, which in turn allowed Virgin's founder, Richard Branson, to fund his Virgin Atlantic airline after coming under stiff competition from arch-rival British Airways. The most important note to take from this – The Smashing Pumpkins were now a major label recording artist.

Before the month was out, the Chicagoans' biggest break yet came courtesy of 'Drown', an eight-minute track included on the *Singles* movie soundtrack.

A romantic comedy set in Seattle around the height of the grunge movement and starring Bridget Fonda, Matt Dillon and Campbell Scott, the soundtrack featured Seattle heroes such as Alice in Chains, Pearl Jam and Soundgarden, and while the Pumpkins were based some two-thousand miles across country, it wasn't hard to see why they had been given a spot on the album on the back of *Gish*'s content.

Written a short time after *Gish* and recorded at Lenny Kravitz's Waterfront Studios in Hudson, New York, 'Drown' is a masterful number that is shrouded in guitar feedback and grungy nuances. Memorable for its extensive solo and utilising feedback in an atmospheric way, like The Cure had been so good at exploring, this panoramic track showed hints of a natural progression from the likes of 'Rhinoceros' and 'Window Paine'. Also securing strong radio traction, Billy Corgan was less than happy that 'Drown' failed to receive an official single release:

> We wanted it to be a single, we were pushing for it. I was even willing to make a video. Radio stations were playing it. And when it came time for the third single, they said "Screaming Trees". And I was like, "Screaming Trees??" But what label is Alice in Chains on and what label are the Screaming Trees on? Epic, which is the label that put out the soundtrack. And that's what killed the song.

Despite falling foul of record label politics, 'Drown' still went to 24 on the Alternative Songs chart, the Pumpkins' best position at the time, and it did enough to create a buzz around the band, which was arguably bigger than *Gish* had achieved. It was as if a switch had been flicked, and suddenly, the Pumpkins were being touted as the next Nirvana. *Nevermind* had sent Nirvana international and record labels were already searching for the next big rock band and mega-selling album. Those were big shoes to fill. The Pumpkins were once again being thrown into the grunge category, but anyone with half an ear could tell the quartet were far more expansive, and perhaps Virgin Records perceived this also. Even so, with the hype came intense pressure, and behind the scenes, things were already starting to fall apart in the Pumpkins camp.

D'arcy and James had been romantically involved since the late eighties, but their relationship hit the skids in the summer of 1992. By August, when the band were set to play one of their biggest shows to date at the Reading Festival bonanza in England, the couple had parted ways. They were at least able to put their personal differences to one side for the sake of their beloved band, as neither was willing to walk away at such an important period of their musical careers.

If emotional pain was gripping two of the four members, addiction was strangling another. Jimmy's heroin use was beginning to get out of control, and his reliance on the sinister drug would reach a critical point in the months to come. Billy was also fighting his own demons, but more on that shortly.

All things considered, the Reading performance on Saturday, 29 August, was a triumphant one. Playing on the main stage in the middle of the afternoon and part of a bill that included Therapy?, Rollins Band, Manic Street Preachers, and the headlining Public Enemy, The Smashing Pumpkins took the chance afforded to them by rifling through a set that contained early versions of some new songs, plus *Gish* highlights such as 'I Am One' and 'Siva'. Reading Festival 1992 will forever be remembered for Nirvana's historic headline slot on the Sunday evening, though, and no one knew it at the time, but it would be the trio's final ever show in the UK. Kurt Cobain was brought onto the stage in a wheelchair whilst wearing a hospital gown – an obvious middle finger to the widespread rumours surrounding the frontman's own deteriorating health at the hands of heroin. A little more than eighteen months later, Cobain was dead, and the grunge movement quickly subsided with his tragic passing.

There was no time to rest for The Smashing Pumpkins. They needed to build on the momentum provided by *Gish* and 'Drown', and the only way to do that was by getting straight to work on a new studio album. It wasn't going to be easy, but the results would give the quartet the platform to become one of the biggest rock bands in the world.

Siamese Dream (1993)

Personnel:
Billy Corgan: lead vocals, guitar, bass
James Iha: guitar
D'arcy Wretzky: bass
Jimmy Chamberlin: drums
Recorded at Triclops Sound Studios, Marietta, Georgia (December 1992-March 1993)
Produced by: Butch Vig, Billy Corgan
Record label: Virgin
Release date: 27 July 1993
Chart positions: UK: 4, US: 10
Running time: 62:08

> We were coming from an alternative universe where if you got lucky, you
> became Sonic Youth and could sell out a club like the Metro. And if you
> were really lucky, you were Echo & the Bunnymen or Depeche Mode
> and could play to 3000 people. That was the world we were living in and
> understood. Then suddenly, Nirvana's blowing up and Pearl Jam's blowing
> up – and don't forget we've been on tour with Red Hot Chili Peppers with
> Pearl Jam opening for us. We saw what was happening and suddenly you
> saw this massive tide coming in, or going out, depending on how you look
> at it. I'm not a stupid guy, so I thought, I better learn how to write some pop
> songs now. You could see that the bands that survived were the ones that
> had actual good songs. My attitude was, I'm not going back to work at the
> record store.
> Billy Corgan

Come the final quarter of 1992, Nirvana and Pearl Jam were the undisputed
kings of the American alt rock scene. *Nevermind* was still shifting huge
numbers – 300,000 copies per week at one point, and it had also topped the
Billboard 200 thanks in no small part to the anthem for a new generation, the
rebellious 'Smells Like Teen Spirit'.

Pearl Jam's meteoric rise didn't happen overnight. Instead, a consistent
set of hard-rocking singles helped the band's debut opus, *Ten*, climb the US
album chart to a peak position of Two – a full year after its release. Pearl Jam
were also credited with leading alt rock's onslaught on the mainstream, and
with the more recent emergence of Stone Temple Pilots and Alice in Chains
especially, who would also sell records in their droves, the pressure was
enough to send Billy Corgan spiralling into a debilitating depression. 'Within
a short span of time, I went from thinking I was very successful within my
given field, to all the rules had changed in my given field', he told Amy Jo
Martin's *Why Not Now?* podcast in 2019. 'Everything I had built myself up
to be and do was no longer as relevant as it needed to be', he continued. 'I

went into a very strange depression because I felt like something had been not taken, but the change made me feel kind of inadequate in a way I wasn't prepared for.'

With Corgan's depression came severe writer's block, and with severe writer's block came thoughts of suicide, to the point where he began to get rid of his personal belongings, and even plotted his own funeral. Thankfully, the frontman was able to rescue the situation in frankly stupendous fashion, and with a 'Shit or Bust' mind frame, write one of The Smashing Pumpkins' biggest ever songs in the process. It's amazing what one can do when their back is against the wall.

The quartet regrouped with Butch Vig and hit Triclops Sound Studios in December 1992. Located in Marietta, Georgia, and just twenty miles from . the state capital, Atlanta, the studio was principally chosen so the band could avoid Chicagoan friends and other distractions while they laid down album number two. More importantly, the move was intended to keep Jimmy Chamberlin off heroin and away from his dealers, but it didn't work. 'Within 24 hours, Jimmy knew every drug dealer, hooker, bookie, and nut case in Atlanta', Vig reminisced sometime later. Also looking back on that period in a subsequent interview, Chamberlin discussed how a young band such as the Pumpkins were more likely to fall foul to a music business blinded by dollar signs, and with no real consideration for a band's welfare:

We were out of our minds. There were drugs, egos, misinformation, and that era of the record business certainly didn't help anybody. There wasn't any emotional management going on. We were just left to our own devices to either deal with it, get lucky, or do something destructive. Unfortunately, there was a lot of destruction going on.

The brilliant but tormented drummer would repeatedly disappear from the studio for days on end, partaking in benders that left the rest of his crew fearing for his life. After an attempted intervention of sorts, Chamberlin was eventually persuaded to check himself into rehab before it was too late.

Another reason Triclops became the studio of choice was because of its Neve 8068 soundboard. John Lennon had previously recorded his final studio album, *Double Fantasy*, with the vintage console at Hit Factory in New York City. Primed for use by rock bands in particular, the console was perfect for the Pumpkins, who were going for a big and fat sound in their music. *Siamese Dream* was recorded entirely on analogue tape and the process was excruciatingly time-consuming. Vig and Corgan once again bounced ideas off one another and like *Gish* before it, the Pumpkins' sophomore effort became a lavish affair, high in production, and extremely dense in content. Because of countless delays, even working twelve hours a day for six days in a row wasn't enough to get things back on schedule. For the final two months, working fifteen-hour days was for the greater good as Vig and especially

Corgan refused to cut corners if it meant the album was going to suffer in doing so, much to the annoyance of Virgin Records bosses whose impatience increased day by day. The album also ended up going over budget by $250,000, but the art would win out on this occasion.

While holed up at Triclops, the group witnessed first-hand the so-called 'Storm of the Century', which hit Georgia on 13 March having formed over the Gulf of Mexico the day before. At its height stretching from Canada to Honduras, recording 100mph winds and snowfall of up to 140cm, the storm would claim the lives of over 300 people and cause over $5 million worth of damage during its three-day assault. A couple of photographs exist online, either taken by Billy or Jimmy, from inside the recording studio and looking out the front door at the snow-covered ground.

Further pressure had been put on Corgan to write more material than he did for *Gish*. 1993 would be the first year since the Compact Disc was invented in which the format would outsell both vinyl and cassettes, and so Virgin pushed the Pumpkins to fill more of the 80-alloted minutes a CD could hold. A 62-minute album wasn't a bad return, considering its leading writer had lost all creativity just a few months prior.

Succeeding in the label's demand came at a cost, though, as Corgan took it upon himself to lay down a lot of the guitar and bass parts, as he had on *Gish*. Able to record the parts easier and in fewer takes was handy to save a bit of time, but James and D'arcy were less impressed at having to take another back seat while their perfectionist dictator took complete control. Corgan also overdubbed his parts on top of some of theirs, which didn't improve the situation either.

The final mix was done by Alan Moulder, because Vig and Corgan were too 'emotionally exhausted' to do it themselves. Moulder had mixed My Bloody Valentine's *Loveless* album and it was for that reason his services were required here, and upon completion, the long-awaited album was finally finished.

Siamese Dream was released on 27 July 1993, receiving universal acclaim from music critics who cited its complex arrangements, its lofty production, and the multi-faceted styles and sounds incorporated into its hour-plus running time. Less in line with many of the grunge releases, which were buoyed on by punk rock energy, *Siamese Dream* leaned towards heavy metal, if anything in its harsher moments. Throwing in some dreamy pop and already tried and tested shoegaze/psychedelia, here was one of the most ostentatious rock albums to arrive in all of 1993.

Debuting at ten on the *Billboard* 200 and hitting the top five in the UK, The Smashing Pumpkins were indeed America's next hottest rock export. Music videos for the album's singles would be featured all over TV, radio stations relentlessly played the songs, and music moguls took enough notice to include *Siamese Dream* in the nominations for the Best Alternative Music Performance (previously known as Best Alternative Music Album) category at the 1994 GRAMMY Awards. The Bono-fronted Irish rockers U2 would take home the gong for their eighth album, *Zooropa*, but also being pitted against Belly, Nirvana, and R.E.M. showed the company the Pumpkins could expect to keep as their career well and truly hit lift-off.

Siamese Dream has since been certified 4x platinum in America and 6x platinum worldwide. Not bad for an album created by a band on the verge of self-destruction for much of its writing and recording cycle.

'Cherub Rock' (Corgan)

One of the last songs written for *Siamese Dream* and in just 30 minutes, according to its creator, the pulsing intro of 'Cherub Rock' fully justifies why it was chosen to open the album.

From the marching-like drums, supposedly a direct lift from part of Rush's four-segue epic, 'By-Tor and the Snow Dog', which give way to James Iha's wiry riff and D'arcy's humming bass, the tension purposefully builds towards a euphoric first explosion of distortion. The Smashing Pumpkins had returned bigger and better than ever, and in less than one minute, they had managed to separate themselves from any and all potential Nirvana comparisons. Media hype and bandwagon hoppers of the indie rock scene had left a bad taste in Billy Corgan's mouth and 'Cherub Rock' was his response – however, his approach was less scathing and more sarcastic. 'Hipsters unite, come align for the big fight to rock for you,' he sings in both defiance and triumph, his vocals going back and forth between tender whispers, angst-ridden whines, and piercing shrieks. 'Who wants honey, as long as there's some money' he retorts on an overly melodic chorus made for both radio and arenas alike, arguably bigger and bolder than any song the band had recorded on *Gish*. Time and experience was already paying off.

Multiple solos spice things up further, breathless and unapologetic in their punchy deliveries. Adding a prominent effect which was achieved by recording the solos to two separate tapes, they were then run together but with one of the tapes at a slightly faster tempo. This was just the first example of pushing the boundaries of what could be done in a recording studio, and with no use of Pro Tools in sight.

Virgin execs were calling for 'Today' to be the album's lead single, but Corgan pushed for 'Cherub Rock'. In fact, he insisted on 'Cherub Rock', and he got his way. Released a month ahead of *Siamese Dream* to whet fans' appetites, the track received some moderate success when it charted on *Billboard*'s Alternative Airplay (7), Modern Rock Tracks (23), and the singles chart in the UK (31). Later in the year, the Pumpkins were the musical guests on the October 30 episode of *Saturday Night Live*, where they performed 'Cherub Rock' to strong applause.

Despite their less than impressive encounter working with Kevin Kerslake on the 'I Am One' music video two years prior, the band gave the director another chance for the 'Cherub Rock' music video. Shot entirely on Super 8 film, a moderate budget meant the quartet were limited as to what they could do in visually representing the song, and so they resorted to performing in a forest setting where Kerslake used certain techniques that gave off a retro and seemingly low-budget feel. Various colour schemes were used throughout to incorporate psychedelic elements to the clip, but the final edit failed to convince Corgan that a second collaboration with Kerslake was going to turn out any better than the first. The video wasn't shelved like 'I Am One' had been, but Corgan soon declared he would never work with Kerslake again.

'Cherub Rock' is a mammoth album opener, and while it may not have been quite so well received as 'Today', the second single, the song has matured like a fine wine in the years since. In the same year *Siamese Dream* was nominated for a GRAMMY, 'Cherub Rock' received a nod in the Best Hard Rock Performance category alongside AC/DC and their live take of the trailblazing 'Highway to Hell', Led Zeppelin icon Robert Plant ('Calling to You'), New York rockers Living Colour ('Leave It Alone'), and the fast-rising Stone Temple Pilots. On this occasion, the Pilots claimed the glory with their unsettling grunge anthem, 'Plush'.

Loud, proud, and hard rocking to the end, 'Cherub Rock' would help The Smashing Pumpkins prepare to transition out of the club scene and into bigger venues more fitting of their multi-dimensional music. The song also offered early reassurance that alternative rock could still thrive beyond Nirvana, should the trio burn out, as many had been predicting since mid-1992. The cynics would ultimately be proven right ...

'Quiet' (Corgan)

Incessant, convulsive, bruising, 'Quiet' is anything but what its title suggests. If 'Cherub Rock' offered a guiding hand into a mainstream willing to accept The Smashing Pumpkins with open arms, 'Quiet' slams the door shut and rescinds the invitation because of the menacing incursion of disorienting and distorted riffs befitting of the backstory, which bore the song's existence.

Documenting Corgan's fraught relationship with his parents and a childhood often bereft of love, this is an eye-opening foray into the frontman's formative years with a heroin-addicted blues musician for a father, and a mother who suffered a mental breakdown and absconded before young Billy was five years old. When his father would go on tour with his band, a new stepmother would physically abuse Billy, and those memories encompass much of what 'Quiet' came to be.

'For years I've been sleeping helpless, couldn't tell a soul,' sings a hostile and condemning Corgan, venting further through crunching alt metal riffs where his fingers work overtime. 'Be ashamed at the mess you've made, my eyes will never forget,' he continues with more turbulence than a plane ride from hell.

When Corgan needs support, he finds it in Jimmy Chamberlin, the drumming just as searing and littered with breathtaking fills. You just know something more anarchic is coming, and when the two duel against each other during a resonant guitar solo, neither man deserves to lose this explicit battle. Music is the real winner.

'It still has a nice adrenaline to it, an icy sheen that gets over because it does ask for excessive quiet while giving none at all', said Corgan when discussing the song in later liner notes. Not many would have foreseen 'Quiet' coming so high up the tracklisting, but The Smashing Pumpkins were never ones for traditionalism.

'Today' (Corgan)

Every rock fan knows this song from its iconic high-pitched, one-measure riff intro. 'Today' is the song that, without sounding too dramatic, saved Billy Corgan's life. At the point of no return, his time on this earth appeared to be coming to an end, and then everything changed:

> I woke up one morning, and I kind of stared out the window and thought, 'Okay, well, if you're not going to jump out the window, you better do whatever it is you need to do.' That morning I wrote 'Today'. It's sort of a wry observation on suicide, but in essence, the meditation behind the lyric is that every day is the best day if you let it be.

The genius of 'Today' is its ballad form. Musically upbeat, pop structured and with a refined tempo, it is a song so well written that many a listener failed to grasp the true meaning of it even though the subject matter was staring them straight in the face.

'Today is the greatest day I've ever known, can't live for tomorrow, I might not have that long' is not a happy line, and neither is the heart-breaking but beautifully poetic sequence of 'Pink ribbon scars that never forget, I tried so hard to cleanse these regrets. My angel wings were bruised and restrained, my belly stings.' But again, Corgan was laying all his cards on the table to tell the world, 'This is me, I'm not okay, but I will be.'

The song fluctuates between soft verses and semi-distorted hooks, the singalong chorus allowing you to imagine a million emotional teenagers singing it in tandem at some kind of alt rock church service. It isn't a long stretch to say that 'Today' became a core anthem in defining the youth of the '90s, not in a dissimilar way to how 'Smells Like Teen Spirit' reacted upon its arrival in 1991. 'Today' is certainly a worthy companion piece.

Virgin chose not to release the song as a single in America, surprisingly, as they wanted people to go out and buy *Siamese Dream* and listen to it in its entirety, but 'Today' was powerful enough in its promo presence that radio stations couldn't get enough of it. Becoming the Pumpkins' highest-charting track at that point, it reached 4 on the Modern Rock Tracks chart and 28 on Mainstream Rock Tracks, while in the UK, where 'Today' did get an official single release, it peaked at 44.

For a music video that almost became as memorable as the song it was promoting, the quartet joined forces with Stephane Sednaoui to create a vibrant and entertaining clip. Corgan discussed the treatment, which he devised after remembering back to his childhood when the local ice cream man decided to quit his day job, so he drove around the neighbourhood giving free ice cream to all the children.

The video begins in the same way, Corgan is now the ice cream man, and after giving away his stock, he takes his truck into the countryside. Picking up James, D'arcy and Jimmy along the way, before long, the four are painting the truck, and themselves, in any colour imaginable, making for a rather messy finale. *MTV* put the video on frequent rotation, which in turn only enhanced the Pumpkins' popularity. 'Today' was also performed on the band's visit to *Saturday Night Live*, along with 'Cherub Rock' as previously mentioned.

Regardless of its dark lyricism, 'Today' is a tale of survival and perseverance, a true The Smashing Pumpkins classic and one of the biggest rock songs of the decade. In the years since its release, Billy Corgan has never forgotten its importance to both himself, and his band:

> The song that changed my life more than any other. The ultimate in irony, a chirpy song about my near-suicide that all the kids sing along to. Probably would not have been a hit if I had offed myself in the gloaming before its release, but one can still ponder past the graveyard.

'Hummer' (Corgan)

At almost seven minutes, 'Hummer' is the second-longest track on *Siamese Dream* and it is more of a collage of ideas rather than a typical verse-chorus-verse kind of song. There is very little recycling of melodies or chord sequences, but still, the effort flows nicely through powerful displays of the quiet/loud dynamic.

'Hummer' touches on Corgan's writer's block and how at one point, he found it impossible to find any inspiration. There are some positive lines thrown in here and there, notably when hinting at the clearing of his brain fog – 'When I woke up from that sleep, I was happier than I'd ever been'. The relief in that line is palpable.

Offering the idea that 'life is not designed for those who are cheerful, whistling, daydreamers, but designed to be cruel and mean', in Corgan's own words, the instrumentation suggests something other than illusions of false hope. The recording includes over 40 tracks, and 'Hummer' is musically both tuneful and buoyant.

Guitar-heavy (of course) but exuding positivity instead of pessimism. The crowning moment comes in its extended playout, where a soothing and almost apparitional section of delicate guitar, bass and drum patterns coagulate to take a slightly psychedelic turn.

'To be yourself, you must live your life. To live your life, you must be free', wrote Corgan in the liner notes of the album's 2011 reissue, clearly feeling much better about life in the years since the inception of 'Hummer'.

'Rocket' (Corgan)

A straightforward arena rocker but with a kind of innocent charm to it, 'Rocket' is not unlike 'Today' in the way that it offers a lighter atmosphere on top of some darker subject matter.

Although it was the first song written for *Siamese Dream*, actually appearing in live sets during the touring of *Gish* but on those occasions featuring random sets of lyrics yet to be finalised, this version of 'Rocket' further points towards Corgan's declining mental health during late '91/early '92. 'The moon is out, the stars invite, I think I'll leave tonight' seems to indicate those suicidal thoughts were still prominent, while 'I torch my soul to show the world I am pure' finds a singer still longing to be accepted. In many ways, though, 'Rocket' reveals Corgan's journey to redemption, the triumphant and repeated rallying cry of 'I shall be free' decisive in its declaration of coming back from the brink.

Dominated by a penetrating and distorted guitar lead from start to finish, this is an overly melodic number that was chosen to be the fourth single from the album. As with all the heavier tracks *Siamese Dream* had at its disposal, the distorted tone was conceived in an extremely unconventional way, as Butch Vig revealed to *Guitar.com* in a 2020 interview:

The engineer at the studio, Mark Richardson, had a weird lap steel guitar that had this little button you could flick, and it was a distortion unit. I asked him if he could take it out, so he took the thing apart and took out this tiny little box, and we started using that for some of the overdrive. Billy still has it, and just had this most insane buzz, it just would kind of stir your brain right up.

An unorthodox route to take, no doubt, but in this instance, the experimentation only enhances the song's huge wall of sound, as this impressive first half of *Siamese Dream* continues. Released in mid-1994, 'Rocket' was only considered a promo in the US. The UK received a 7" vinyl release, and in Australia, a now highly collectable CD was issued. As with many later singles, chart success was severely limited, and 'Rocket' had a best showing on the Mainstream Rock Tracks chart at 28.

A highly enjoyable video was filmed, where the Pumpkins send an 'Interplanetary Transmission' from outer space to a group of science-loving, tech-savvy kids living in a typical suburban neighbourhood. The kids raid a scrapyard and build their own rocket ship so they can fly to meet the band, but by the time they arrive, they find Corgan and company have severely aged. The video was directed by Jonathan Dayton and Valerie Faris, who would work with some of the biggest rock bands of the decade before moving into feature films.

'Disarm' (Corgan)

And then came a song completely leftfield compared to all that came before it, a surprise to many an unsuspecting listener, a song which would become one of the Pumpkins' boldest and best endeavours.

'Disarm' is dramatic, cinematic, and utterly fascinating, but those sinister undertones return as Billy Corgan revisits his childhood for another attack on the parents he felt had failed him. An acoustic ballad that is eclipsed by orchestral anecdotes, and with tense additions of church bells to boot, a gothic sadness surrounds a song which was written around the same time as 'Today'. Another 'suicidal anthem', as Corgan liked to call it. During an interview with *Rage* magazine in 1993, Corgan discussed how the song came about:

> I didn't have the guts to kill my parents, so I thought I'd get back at them through song. And rather than have an angry, angry, angry, violent song I thought I'd write something beautiful and make them realise what tender feelings I have in my heart, and make them feel really bad for treating me like shit.

Of all the tracks on *Siamese Dream*, 'Disarm' showed Corgan's songwriting progression best, which is why it stands out so far from the crowd. It was originally intended to be a heavy rock song, but Butch Vig struggled to figure out an approach in making it so. Working off Corgan's acoustic demonstration, it is safe to say the version we all know and love is the most perfect form the producer could have come up with. Corgan called in Eric Remschneider and David Ragsdale to add some cello and violin parts, respectively, put together by Corgan singing the envisioned pieces because a score had not been prepared. At this point, 'Disarm' assumed its true identity.

Corgan's lyrics were always going to be unflinching, and being chosen as the third single meant that extra ears would be hearing what the frontman had to say. Naturally, the content was likely to cause a stir with some. The biggest controversy occurred in the UK, where 'Disarm' was banned by *BBC* Radio because of the 'Cut that little child' and 'The killer in me is the killer in you' lines. Released on 21 February 1994, the timing was unfortunate because the nation was still struggling to digest the horrific murder of two-year-old James Bulger twelve months before. Tortured and killed by two ten-year-old boys, the shock and disbelief felt by many was still extremely raw, so it wasn't a complete surprise when Corgan was asked to edit some of the song's lyrics if he wanted 'Disarm' to be played on the radio and be the hit it was projected to be. Corgan declined. 'Disarm' didn't suffer from its lack of exposure, reaching 11 in the UK Singles chart. In America, five on Mainstream Rock Tracks and eight on Alternative Airplay were strong results, and the Pumpkins' rise continued.

By now, the band's music videos were also becoming more sophisticated, and the Jake Scott-directed clip for 'Disarm' was the most artistic yet. Mostly filmed in black and white, the band members' performances are superimposed over aerial shots of a gothic church-like building. There is some small usage of colour film showing a small boy playing outside (an innocent portrayal of a young Corgan?), as well as a man slowly moving through an underpass to add further subplots. There may not have ever been much of a story to the band's videos, but there were often scenes relative to certain parts of the song's lyrics.

'Disarm' spent a month being billed as *MTV*'s 'Exclusive Video', and later in 1994, it was nominated for Best Alternative Video and Best Editing in a Video at the *MTV* Video Music Awards. Nirvana's 'Heart-Shaped Box' won the first of those categories, and R.E.M.'s 'Everybody Hurts' won the other. Ironically, it was a win-win for Pat Sheffield, who had edited both the Pumpkins' and R.E.M.'s videos.

An electric guitar-driven take has been played on various occasions, most notably at the '94 VMA's, but the studio version cannot be bettered. One of the most-played songs on US radio that year, 'Disarm' was another pivotal moment for both the Pumpkins and alternative rock, in the process tearing up the rulebook on what a traditional rock song should sound like.

'Soma' (Corgan, Iha)

Inspired by his break-up with then-girlfriend Chris Fabian, Billy gets creative on a near seven-minute opus, which starts off soft and psychy and builds nicely towards the same distorted heaviness people were coming to expect across much of the album's tracklisting.

Titled 'Coma' in its early days, 'Soma' finds Corgan numbing himself as a way to cope with his relationship breakdown. Readers of classic literature will be able to find a correlation to Aldous Huxley's 1932 novel *Brave New World*, in which the author introduces the Soma drug to block out feelings of pain, grief and anger – therefore, everyone walks around in a hazy state of happiness.

'Based on the idea that a love relationship is almost the same as opium: it slowly puts you to sleep, it soothes you, and gives you the illusion of sureness and security', described Corgan when debating 'Soma' – underlined by the song's standout lyric, 'The opiate of blame is your broken heart'.

Split into two halves but nicely coming together as one, the track begins slowly and with a lucid piano piece performed by Mike Mills from R.E.M., before tentative guitar, bass and percussion takes over as the scene is further set. James Iha was given a co-writing credit for the chord structure here, before the blisteringly heavy burst that follows was emphasised by the use of up to 40 overdubbed guitars. The most unforgettable moment comes in the form of the emotionally charged guitar solo that runs for over two minutes and well into the third stanza. It was so well-received that *NME* magazine would later rank it in their 50 Greatest Guitar Solos list in 2017, while *Rolling Stone* had included it in their 25 Coolest Guitar Solos list ten years earlier.

The closing line of 'I'm all by myself, as I've always felt. I'll betray myself to anyone' is a sad reminder that all was not well with its writer at the time; however, he and Fabian would soon reunite and go on to get married.

'Geek U.S.A.' (Corgan)

The second side of *Siamese Dream* is welcomed in with the demanding 'Geek U.S.A.', which is a re-working of an older track that Pumpkins die-hards will remember as 'Suicide Kiss'. On this occasion, the original title sounds much cooler.

Delivered at an intense speed and highly complex through the inclusion of some 30 overdubbed guitars, all of which have distinctive sounds that, when combined together, form a paralysing tour de force. This is The Smashing Pumpkins pushing themselves further in a bid for world domination.

Jimmy Chamberlin is the star of the show, his thick beats promoted higher in the mix, and when a wistful interlude changes the mood halfway through, there is room for some polished jazz fills to take centre stage. 'One of the most amazing drum performances I've ever heard' was how Butch Vig described it, and it is hard to disagree as Chamberlin's full repertoire of techniques thrive at one point or another here.

'Geek U.S.A.' clocks in at just over five minutes; however ', Suicide Kiss' ran for over seven. The lyrics are made up of solemn but poetic passages where an overall theme is tough to unmask. In some ways, it feels like a compilation of Billy Corgan musings, acting as afterthoughts to the music, but there is plenty of self-loathing going on as found on the line 'Sear those thoughts of me, alone and unhappy, I never liked me anyway'. Still, it only endears the listener more to this geeky Chicagoan anti-hero.

Another song, another raging guitar solo, but dumbed down on its intricacy compared to the 'Suicide Kiss' take and considerably shorter in length, too. Corgan almost scrapped the solo altogether, feeling it didn't bring anything special to the song's already solidified dynamism; but its presence was fully vindicated when readers of *Guitar World* magazine named it their 54th greatest guitar solo. High praise indeed.

'Mayonaise' (Corgan, Iha)

As this book goes to press, *Siamese Dream* has celebrated its 30th anniversary, and it sounds as spirited today as it did all the way back in 1993. And then you consider the songs, collectively launching The Smashing Pumpkins into rock's elite but one by one possessing enough power and influence to stand on their own two feet. The word 'Classic' gets thrown around far too often and erroneously a lot of the time, but in this instance ', Cherub Rock', 'Today' and 'Disarm' are more than deserving of such a tag. Their impact on the '90s rock scene simply cannot be denied.

Just when you think *Siamese Dream* has peaked and the remaining songs will crawl towards a safer finale, 'Mayonaise' tiptoes in with a gentle and introspective guitar line and all ears are re-engaged with increased intrigue. A heaviness is still there in the song but at a reserved level, its melodicism veering into ballad terrain but presenting a kind of absorbing fascination not seen at any other point on the album.

There weren't many high-profile grunge and alt rock acts who didn't throw a ballad in here and there, a sure-fire way to light up the radio airwaves and likely obtain a hit record in the process. Soundgarden had 'Black Hole Sun', the Red Hot Chili Peppers had the lush drug anthem, 'Under the Bridge', and the Stone Temple Pilots had the GRAMMY-winning 'Plush'. You could even include Nirvana in the conversation with the starkly prophetic 'Come as You Are', in which Kurt Cobain swore he didn't have a gun; and then Bush emerged in 1994 with the silky smooth 'Glycerine'. These were great bands with great songs, but they were not The Smashing Pumpkins, and they didn't have 'Mayonaise'.

Its title simply comes from Corgan staring into his fridge, but choosing to spell it a slightly different way (a play on the phrase 'My Own Eyes' has also been rumoured over the years), 'Mayonaise' is a stunning and musically enthralling number containing all the key components of '90s radio rock – even though it wasn't actually released as a single. And that is why the song has such immeasurable charm.

There is a vagueness to the lyrics that is caused by, in Corgan's own words, 'throwing a bunch of weird one-liners together', but it works; so much so that despair and loss are overbearing themes which then extend to love and a romance that fails to blossom. 'Fool enough to almost be it, cool enough to not quite see it, doomed' feels autobiographical, touching on Corgan's recent relationship woes. 'We'll try and ease the pain, but somehow we'll feel the same. Well, no one knows where our secrets go,' is as relatable as it is profound.

'Mayonaise' was the final song written for *Siamese Dream*. James Iha came up with the chords and an instrumental demo before he and Corgan worked on an arrangement that was beautifully crafted into six minutes of utter perfection. A less extravagant guitar solo still sounds huge, while squealing high notes stem from a cheap guitar Corgan was using. When he would stop playing, he found the guitar would emit strange whistling sounds, so he decided to write some pieces that purposely had abrupt finishes, so the whistling could become part of the song.

There is no doubt that 'Today' and 'Disarm' particularly elevated the quartet's mainstream status, but we will never know what would have happened had 'Mayonaise' been chosen as the fourth single instead of 'Rocket'. 'Rocket' is an excellent song, without doubt, but 'Mayonaise' is on a whole other level. In a 2012 interview, Corgan spoke about putting lyrics to the song. He didn't realise it at the time, but perhaps subconsciously, there was some method in his madness:

It didn't feel like it had any synchronicity to me; I was just looking for good lines to sing. And now, when I sing the song, I'm just shocked at how closely reflective it is of what I was going through. It's almost like this weird personal anthem, to my experience, but it didn't feel that way at the time.

'Spaceboy' (Corgan)

Next up is a loving ode from Billy to his younger half-brother, Jesse, who was born with a mild form of cerebral palsy, Tourette's, and a chromosomal disorder. Early on, there was a fear Jesse would never be able to walk or talk, but a comfortable life under difficult circumstances was provided by the Corgan family as he managed to gain a good degree of independence as he got older.

'Spaceboy' details the struggles of fitting in with or without any ailments, like Billy himself also dealt with. An acoustic-driven song and discharging a sweet innocence, Corgan also brought a Mellotron in for a cameo appearance – a piece of kit first manufactured in the UK in the early 1960s and the first type of sampler made available on the music market. Here, the Mellotron provides some tender orchestral movements to reinforce the sombre nature of the content, while the rest of the band are relegated to playing minimal roles.

'We don't belong' is a repeated line covered in a bleak realness, but the positive side of the story is that both brothers went on to create good lives for themselves, which may not have seemed likely in their younger years. Perhaps the power of overcoming the odds is the message to take from 'Spaceboy', because, song-wise, it is one of the weaker efforts found on this record.

'Silverfuck' (Corgan)

At nearly nine minutes long, the brilliantly titled 'Silverfuck' is the longest track on *Siamese Dream*. Written a good two years before reaching the masses, it very much feels like you are witnessing a live jam session. In fact, the Pumpkins first performed 'Silverfuck' during a show in Philadelphia on 18 July 1991.

Fast, frantic and abundantly metallic, the first third refuses to let up as seething riffs and colossal drum sections force an attack on the senses. It's as if the band members are possessed at this stage, but then, out of nowhere, another dreamy interlude changes the song's trajectory, a calm replacing the chaos. Corgan's whispered vocal swoons over faint guitar flutters, deft cymbal rides, and minimalistic bass, as the frontman repeats the line 'I feel no pain' in a section focusing on lost love. Dystopia is restored for part three, a frantic assault where Corgan shouts 'Bang bang you're dead, hole in the head' as the instrumentation builds to a frenzy. A prolonged outro of dissonant distortion and guitar feedback brings the end of a rock concert to mind, where the cymbals thrash and crash, and the guitar strings are ravaged by bleeding fingertips.

Over the years, 'Silverfuck' has become the Pumpkins' most-played album track in the live environment. The song has also been manipulated and experimented on, sometimes having the lead riffs removed entirely and replaced with ambient textures. Commonly, it has been extended to last for over twenty minutes, and during the band's 'final' show at the Metro in 2000, a 35-minute version of 'Silverfuck' was performed. One day, the track may go for even longer, as Corgan hinted in the 2011 reissue liner notes:

An endless jam that we beat into submission, using the club crowds as test dummies for what needs to be an ever-infinite magnum opus ... Eventually, this song will stretch in 45 minutes, driving half the crowd for the exits.

'Sweet Sweet' (Corgan)
A brief intermission-like singalong containing thick layers of chorus set acoustic guitar, subtle shaker percussion, and little else. 'Sweet Sweet' comes across as a Corgan solo track, running for just over 90 seconds as he sings a small refrain surrounding a love he knows he should not be pursuing. 'I'll take, take, take all that you have for me, in sin, where are we going?' he smoothly protests before things draw to a quick close.

'Luna' (Corgan)
In the early '90s, Billy briefly dated Courtney Love. A wild child who often made the headlines for all the wrong reasons, the Hole singer soon moved on to Kurt Cobain, whom she would marry, have a child with, and share a heroin addiction with.

At some point, Love came out and arrogantly stated that most of the lyrics on *Siamese Dream* had been written about her, and while that is clearly untrue when you listen to 'Quiet', 'Geek U.S.A.', 'Silverfuck' even, she is likely to have at least been correct about 'Luna'. 'I'm in love with you, so in love', declares a wounded Corgan, who then admits to being under a spell he cannot break. When 'Luna' was written, he would also have been missing Chris Fabian, but his liner notes for the album's reissue appear to confirm that Courtney was indeed his inspiration for this one, while also providing a small dig at the same time:

I am in love with someone that doesn't love me. My songs are better than hers. This is my way to prove a point not worth making.

Continuing on from the mellow tone set by 'Sweet Sweet', 'Luna' closes a masterful album with a true love ballad. Eric Remschneider and David Ragsdale return with some heart-warming string arrangements as a sitar-like guitar and zephyr drumming flows from start to finish. In a sense, 'Luna' is a slightly underwhelming song compared to everything that came before it, but detached it showed the Pumpkins had an affectionate side when they chose to expose it. And with 'Luna' came the end to *Siamese Dream*, regularly regarded as one of the greatest rock albums of not just the '90s, but of all time.

Pisces Iscariot (1994)

Personnel:
Billy Corgan: lead vocals, guitar
James Iha: guitar, lead vocals, backing vocals
D'arcy Wretzky: bass, backing vocals
Jimmy Chamberlin: drums
Recorded at: Smart Studios, Madison, Wisconsin, Triclops Sound Studios, Marietta, Georgia, Soundworks Studio, Chicago, Illinois, Maida Vaile Studios, London, England (1991-1993)
Recorded by: Billy Corgan, Butch Vig, Kerry Brown, Dale Griffin
Record label: Virgin
Release date: 4 October 1994
Chart positions: US: 4, NZ: 2, UK:96
Running time: 57:26

The Pumpkins' extensively toured *Siamese Dream* from the summer of 1993, through to September of the following year. Along the way, they made various TV appearances, including an acoustic set for *MTV* at their London studio, and the quartet took the then-known Verve on the road for a UK run – long before the Wigan indie rockers hit it big with the songs 'Bittersweet Symphony', and 'The Drugs Don't Work'. The two bands were labelmates in the UK, having both been on the Hut Recordings roster. On a gruelling two-part US trek, the Pumpkins' played anywhere and everywhere with national rock acts such as Red Red Meat, Shudder to Think, and Swervedriver. The Chicago four weren't quite ready for the arena setting just yet, but crowds continued to increase while *Siamese Dream* continued to sell in its droves. By March 1994, the album had already been certified double platinum in America.

And then the musical landscape changed forever when, on 8 April, Kurt Cobain was found dead in his own home from a self-inflicted shotgun wound to the head. Nirvana was no more, and the grunge movement soon subsided in both the wake of Cobain's death, and from the scene's other protagonists experimenting with different styles of rock. Out went grunge and in returned heavy metal, awaking from its slumber and rearing its ugly head through the emergence of Machine Head, and Korn in particular, who were feeding off the mainstream success of the Metallicas and Panteras and bringing a new kind of rage to the devil's favourite noise.

Just a short time ago, The Smashing Pumpkins were being touted as the next Nirvana and now they had little choice but to step up to the plate and lead a second alt rock charge. Their lofty status was solidified when the quartet were given the headline slot on the year's two-month Lollapalooza festival, which had ironically been offered to Nirvana with a reported $10 million payday for the trio. Nirvana had actually officially turned down the gig the day before Cobain's body was found. Topping a bill that included the Beastie Boys, A Tribe Called Quest, Nick Cave and the Bad Seeds, and rising punks Green Day, this was the break Corgan and company had been waiting for, even if they got it under rather unfortunate circumstances. At the turn of the year, the band also took part in the six-date Big Day Out festival, held across Australia and New Zealand. Joining the Ramones, Soundgarden, Primus, Björk and The Breeders, all the hard work that had gone into *Siamese Dream* was beginning to pay dividends.

When it came to music, Billy Corgan has always been a complete workaholic. Writing song after song for every album cycle, many of them would be discarded and left unreleased. In between *Siamese Dream* and a prospective third studio album, Corgan decided to open the vault and pick a selection of tracks for a compilation with the early working title of *Neptulius*, but later officially named *Pisces Iscariot*.

On 4 October, a first VHS tape was released, *Vieuphoria*, featuring live performances from European and American shows on the *Siamese Dream* world tour. To coincide with *Vieuphoria*, *Pisces Iscariot* was released on the same day, its contents presenting a set of songs that many a listener could not fathom how or why they had been lying dormant for so long. The tracklisting appeared carefully thought out, in such a way that both the acoustic and heavy rock songs cohesively flowed without ever settling into periods of slumber.

The album outperformed *Siamese Dream* by going straight in at four on the *Billboard* 200 – in the same week that R.E.M. rocketed to number one with their ninth album, *Monster*. It took just six weeks for *Pisces* to sell a million copies in the US. Strangely, it didn't fare as well in the UK, although it did have a delayed release by a couple of weeks, which could have been a likely reason for only scoring a 96 in the country's album chart.

Pisces Iscariot has been widely considered one of the Pumpkins' finest-ever releases, proving that sometimes compilations can be so much more than just a bunch of songs being randomly thrown together.

'Soothe' (Corgan)

On both their studio albums up to this point, the Pumpkins had nominated strong opening statements of intent. 'I Am One' and 'Cherub Rock' were built around heavy instrumentation and an energy that immediately set the scene for what else was to come, but with *Pisces Iscariot* being more of a venture into the unknown, and all bets were off this time around.

'Soothe' is the polar opposite of a traditional rock album opener, the title fitting this warm-hearted acoustic ballad, where the guitar is the only instrument used here. What makes 'Soothe' so seductive is its origins, recorded by Corgan in his own apartment around Spring 1992. Capturing the exact moment of its conception, this is how Corgan envisioned the song to be, stripped bare of any kind of editing had the recording taken place in a studio. A snapshot of a moment in time where exquisite melodies effervesce over a small set of lost love lyrics, underscored by the mournful line of 'I'll miss you, I don't wish you hurt, I forgive you, I don't wish you away'. It is hard not to like 'Soothe' for what it is, even if it isn't particularly spectacular, but its charisma comes from its purity and its revealing of a musician sitting lonely in his apartment with a guitar in his hands, willing to put his heartache to song and tape.

Corgan considered including 'Soothe' on *Siamese Dream,* but he admitted to 'wimping out' of the idea. It was probably a good idea because it would have been overshadowed by the majority of the other songs on the album. At least here and being the first track, 'Soothe' is given the attention it deserves.

'Frail and Bedazzled' (Corgan)

In March 1992, the Pumpkins entered Kerry Brown's Soundworks Studio in Chicago to record some new demos. They didn't intend to do anything else with them, but when Virgin asked the band to provide some B-sides to go on future single releases, a handful of the demos were worked into full songs and some of them are found scattered throughout *Pisces Iscariot.* 'Frail and Bedazzled' is the first.

Exhibiting the quartet's progression between *Gish* and *Siamese Dream* and appearing to find them leaving their psychedelic influences behind, 'Frail and Bedazzled' sparks a feisty return with churning and distorted guitars, groove-laden bass, and typically vibrant drumming. *Gish* may have earned the Pumpkins some moderate success, but Billy Corgan was living in a parking garage at the time of writing this song's lyrics, which ironically find him battling to adapt to his newfound fame. 'And all I wanted was to be happy, and since I've gave up, I'm free' he sings with a familiar snarl, before suggesting fame and fortune will not replace the loneliness he is longing to rid himself of. 'Their love has failed,' he later sighs, a capella.

As this excellent rocker continues at speed, it seems inconceivable that 'Frail and Bedazzled' was considered nothing more than B-side worthy; however, its omission becomes understandable due to its lack of correlation to the albums it was written between. We should probably thank Virgin Records for wanting more material, or else this one may never have surfaced. Three separate but equally powerful guitar solos authenticate the song further, before Corgan produces one of his most projecting lines of discomfort: 'Frail and bedazzled from all the glare'. Success was certainly going to come at a personal cost.

'Plume' (Corgan, Iha)

A B-side on the second 'I Am One' single, 'Plume' takes the band's use of distortion and overdrive to murkier depths not before heard. Mid-tempo and almost lazy sounding, you can tell this is an older song where the stoner-like guitar fuzz separates 'Plume' from everything the four had come up with thus far.

This is not a throwaway song, far from it, and it even contains one of Corgan's favourite-ever lyrics. 'My boredom has outshined the sun, it's so down low,' he sings on a short chorus, the line reportedly written while he was stuck in an airport with plenty of time to kill.

In the liner notes, the frontman mentions James Iha bringing an outline of 'Plume' to the table, before demoing the song and adding it to the pile of potential tracks for *Siamese Dream*. Iha's involvement is interesting because nowhere else has he ever been acknowledged as being a co-writer of this one. Two screeching solos epitomise the whole feel of 'Plume', the second especially appearing adventurous in its prolonged capacity. The Smashing Pumpkins rarely sounded as ragged as this ever again.

'Whir' (Corgan)
Another to be recorded during the *Siamese* sessions but intentionally for a B-side only, 'Whir' was completed in just one hour and it is evident the band wanted to quickly move on from this one.

Iha's spacey guitar creates some nice riff structures which overthrow Corgan's acoustic lead, but as the definition of the title suggests, there is a languid formula which protrudes throughout the whole of the four-minute running time. D'arcy's simple bass plucking and Jimmy's softly brushed drumming fails to flatter, and after the enjoyable spurt of 'Frail and Bedazzled' and 'Plume', 'Whir' feels like a small step backwards. Corgan does bring some solid lyricism inspired by love and the fear that comes from it; in fact, the line 'She says she wants to marry me, she says she wants a baby, it's not easy when you're scared' is a saving grace of what is very much a safe and substandard Pumpkins song.

'Blew Away' (Iha)
The first song to appear on an officially released album that is all of James Iha's own work, 'Blew Away' was also a B-side on the *Smile* version of the 'Disarm' single.

From the very first sprightly riff with its country twang, relayed over a clean guitar, it just feels completely different to the style of Billy Corgan's songwriting. Iha's voice is also given full exposure, his clean and hazy vocals that, when combined with the softer strut of the instrumentation, brings the sounds of the sixties to mind – the Beatles, Beach Boys et al.

'Blew Away' is sweet, unthreatening, and offers a break to Corgan's melodrama; a love song which Iha could have written with D'arcy in mind. 'I wanna let her know that I won't let her go, I wanna let her know that I love her so,' he sings with a lump in his throat. The difference between the band's primary songwriters is perfectly highlighted in this very song, and Corgan glowingly praised his counterpart's work in the compilation's liner notes: 'Quiet and cool and whispered. This is a beautiful song. The only song we have ever done that I did not stick my nose into, and I am glad I didn't.'

Head and shoulders above both of the acoustic-orientated songs heard thus far on *Pisces*, 'Blew Away' then takes an unexpected turn when the distorted guitars make a return for a thrilling guitar solo, performed by Corgan instead of Iha, as part of a finale where if this was being played live, every member of the audience would be waving their lighters in unison. Another interesting footnote to 'Blew Away' is that Kerry Brown plays the drums, as Jimmy Chamberlin was on vacation at the time of recording. Brown does a decent job of filling an almost impossible void. A largely unheralded gem in the Pumpkins' canon.

'Pissant' (Corgan)
Just from its title, you can tell 'Pissant' is going to be an angry rocker, and damn, is it heavy too. With time running against the band in the studio, Butch Vig scoffed at the idea the Pumpkins could lay down the song in just three hours. His challenge was accepted, and the mission was successfully accomplished.

Sounding all the more compelling for being recorded live, this is without doubt one of the quartet's most fractious songs. There is a strong industrial feel to Chamberlin's monstrous drumming, and with some schizophrenic guitar playing leading the way, 'Pissant' provides a two-and-a-half-minute frenzied attack capable of shaking its listeners to their very core. There is no clear theme involved because Corgan had just a short time to come up with some lyrics; however, his vocals are immensely powerful in their brash and uncontrolled approach.

Included on the 'Cherub Rock' single, and also on the Japanese edition of *Siamese Dream* but under the tongue-in-cheek title of 'Hikari Express' ('Hikari' means 'Light' in Japanese), 'Pissant' was also pushed to be included on the worldwide album release but Corgan resisted his own temptation as he felt it didn't fit with what was already set to be included. Still, it is a brutally brilliant song.

'Hello Kitty Kat' (Corgan)
A fine snapshot of the moody and visceral side of '90s alt rock, 'Hello Kitty Kat' is an incredible track which still manages to maintain an air of accessibility. One of the standout moments on this entire album, and in Corgan's own words, his most 'passive aggressive' song, a raw but pulsating rhythm section features another defining Chamberlin drum display, crashing and thrashing as if his life depends on it, without a moment's pause for the four-plus minutes the track runs for.

The lyrics heard on this version of 'Hello Kitty Kat' are different from those found on the Soundworks demo, but they are more imaginative and find Corgan revisiting his yearning for love and acceptance, as shown in this glorious passage:

Slit my wrists and die a whore,
love to love to love what you adore,
I can give you anything, but please let me be your everything.

The song is led by a domineering riff enhanced by maximum overdrive, but it is the extended and shrieking solo that puts the cherry on top of the cake. Roaring to an epic climax atop some fiery drum rolls and an outspoken deep bass fill, it is astonishing that 'Hello Kitty Kat' only achieved B-side status, featuring on the 'Today' single. Originally planned to be included on *Siamese Dream*, it was cut at the last minute because Corgan felt he had destroyed the mix. If there was ever a song considered to be a glaring omission from any Pumpkins studio album, 'Hello Kitty Kat' may just be it.

'Obscured' (Corgan)

Found on the UK and Japanese editions of the 'Today' CD single, 'Obscured' actually dates back to the Gish sessions. Instead of being chosen for that album, it was intended to be put on the *Lull* EP, which followed later in 1991, and released as a single. It has never been revealed why neither of those instances occurred, however, and Billy Corgan's only revelation as to why was when he wrote in the Pisces liner notes, 'They tricked me'. Cryptic indeed.

With that said, 'Obscured' is an opulent and tranquil number, slightly overlong at 5:22 but nonetheless understated. Acoustic, but with the addition of a semi-electric guitar with harmonic feedback instilling a nice and dreamy vibe, there is a degree of psychedelic relativity much akin to the time period when the song was birthed.

'Through these eyes, I rely on all I've seen, obscured, through these eyes it looks like I'm home tonight', sings Corgan, his strong vocal occasionally offering moments of self-reflection. There are some sparkling chord progressions and the finely brushed percussion adds further atmosphere, but if there is anything negative to say about 'Obscured' it is its overly long playout which ends with a dose of harsh feedback. There is simply no need for it. Still, this very much remains a fan favourite twenty-plus years later.

'Landslide' (Stevie Nicks)

One of two covers to feature on *Pisces Iscariot*, the first is the charming and solely acoustic rendition of 'Landslide'. The eighth track on Fleetwood Mac's 1975 self-titled album, 'Landslide' was a pivotal moment for Stevie Nicks, who was at a career crossroads at the time of writing the song. Her and boyfriend Lindsey Buckingham's first collaboration album, *Buckingham Nicks*, had been deemed a commercial failure after its 1973 release, and was subsequently dropped by Polydor Records. Disillusioned with the music business, Nicks was weighing up whether to return to school until Buckingham was asked to join the rising Fleetwood Mac in late 1974. He agreed to do so on the proviso that Nicks was brought into the fold, too. And the rest, as they say, is history.

Billy Corgan felt 'Landslide' was relative to his own life, the powerful and contemplative lyrics striking a raw nerve, and he sings the words with passionate repose as he strives to do the cover justice.

Oh mirror in the sky, what is love?
Can the child within my head rise above?
Can I sail through the changing ocean tides?
Can I handle the seasons of my life?'

The lighter finger-picked guitar work finds the Pumpkins' version slower and more intimate than the original, while an overdubbed solo gels nicely into the mix. The song turned out so well that it received Nicks' personal seal of approval.

Recorded on 12 September 1993 at *BBC*'s Egton House in London, this is the only Pumpkins take of 'Landslide' to exist. Also recorded that day was a raw and savage rendition of 'Quiet', 'Disarm', and a cover of Depeche Mode's 'Never Let Me Down Again'. All three tracks were produced by Ted De Bono, however, Corgan was critical of the sound quality and in the album's liner notes, he didn't mince his words on his disdain for the BBC after two poor experiences working with them:

> The recording is way too hissy and we're sorry, but it is the fault of the *BBC*, whose financial raping of us to use this song and 'Sandoz' almost didn't make putting these songs out possible. But it is here.

Little feedback seemed to be given on 'Landslide' when it was included as a B-side on the *Heart* version of the 'Disarm' single, but when promoting *Pisces Iscariot*, Corgan chose to release the cover as a single. No music video was filmed, but the elegance of 'Landslide' still caught mainstream attention and the song reached three on *Billboard*'s Alternative Airplay chart, as well as 30 on the US Radio Songs chart. An unexpected hit it was, and in the process, it became one of the Pumpkins' most adored tracks.

'Starla' (Corgan)

It's easy to drool over the Pumpkins' discography and pick your favourite songs, defining moments, or even points where the band went from potential stars to masters of their craft. 'Silverfuck' was a showcase of their ability in writing longer and dense opuses with dynamics that few of the quartet's contemporaries possessed at the same time; and then 'Starla' emerged and upped the ante even farther.

It would also be interesting to see inside the mind of Billy Corgan to gauge his thought process, his approach to songwriting, and how he comes to the decision of which songs do or do not make the cut, because 'Starla' very much deserved the grandest launch, like how a Hollywood blockbuster gets a red-carpet premiere.

The Smashing Pumpkins thrust themselves into the alt rock scene not by playing things safe, but by presenting an expansive set of songs which made *Gish* the unexpected success it became. The album was still in its infancy when the band entered Soundworks in Spring 1992, and with much of the psych rock leanings now firmly in the rear-view mirror, 'Starla' was one of the tracks recorded during those sessions and many of us would surely love to have been a fly on the wall to witness this one being put to tape.

Completed in a single session to meet a tight deadline, 'Starla' is an eleven-minute marathon and built around an intense and extended guitar solo. Hugely experimental and like 'Silverfuck', sounding like a full-band jam, the sounds and tones emanating from Corgan and Iha's guitars are at times bewildering, and the timely fluctuations of the quiet-loud dynamic hint that this is just the calm before the storm. And that storm comes at the halfway point, when the abrasive solo announces itself in all its glory. Battling the elevated noisescape for control, sometimes appearing victorious and at other moments having to resist and blend in with the heavy procession; but always fighting to make itself heard. The solo gets better at every turn and the fervent wah-distorted lead creates an almighty impact, which many of rock and metal's elite would have been envious of upon first listen.

There are a small set of vocals because the majority of the interest is rightfully spotlighted on the instrumentation, but the song's title is repeatedly mentioned in those brief passages. If you listen closely around the 5:20 point, you will just about be able to hear a police car siren in the background, which was picked up while Corgan was recording his vocals.

The humorous story of how 'Starla' got its name was mentioned by Corgan in the *Pisces* liner notes, when on tour with the Red Hot Chili Peppers, Corgan met a girl in Dallas who told him her name was Starla. Immediately earmarking the name for a future song title, Corgan would then meet the girl a couple of years later, only to find out her name was in fact, Darla.

'Starla' was produced by Kerry Brown, who used a Soundcraft TS12 board to record the song onto a TASCAM MS16 one-inch tape machine – the best kit at his disposal in 1992 and before Pro Tools was more widely integrated into studios. There is a backwards effect implemented across the first third of the track, an Eventide H3000 Ultra-Harmoniser making that possible, and yet 'Starla' was still resigned to B-side level. Fans of the Pumpkins who were based in the UK will most likely have had an enormous eargasm when picking up the 'I Am One' 12" single because not only did they get to hear 'Plume' as a B-side, they were also treated to the incomparable 'Starla' too.

The track has been performed live over 180 times, becoming just as popular as almost any other The Smashing Pumpkins song – and that includes the hit singles. A stunning song written by a band who, at the time, were still young and continuing to learn the rock and roll ropes, 'Starla' found the Pumpkins ready to graduate.

'Blue' (Corgan)

The sad/happy 'Blue' makes its second appearance, having first shown up on the *Lull* EP. Structurally simplistic but uplifting with D'arcy's convincing bass line and the tolling of wind chimes in its intro, 'Blue' glides along with a hardened swagger as Corgan begs the lady in lyrical question to 'stay with me for a while'.

The frontman considered using an acoustic version of the song for this compilation before deciding to stick with the rock mix, and the reflective passage that sees out 'Blue' would likely not have sounded so elegant had it been stripped of its muscle.

'Girl Named Sandoz' (Eric Burdon, Vig Briggs, John Weider, Barry Jenkins, Danny McCulloch)
Even though their experience recording for the *Peel Sessions* and the *BBC*, in general, was not great, the Pumpkins were clearly content with how their cover of 'Landslide', and The Animals' 'Girl Named Sandoz' turned out that they fought hell and high water to be able to release them both. The quartet sound loose, loud and dirty, hitting all the right spots as their pent-up frustration from the recording process is unloaded into a primaeval performance that is worth hearing again and again.

'La Dolly Vita' (Corgan)
Billy Corgan later conceded that 'La Dolly Vita' was written about his mother, and his admission is strongly reinforced by the opening line, which touches on the painful memories of a childhood lost: 'I lay my head on her bosom to cry myself to sleep, I see no greater wisdom that she has given to me.' Instrumentally, this B-side on the original 'Tristessa' single is a fine example of the Pumpkins' early star potential.

'Spaced' (Corgan)
Closing out this phenomenal compilation album is a rather bizarre piece which appears to be an experiment in audio manipulation. The guitar line may be quite pensive, but Corgan's overdubbed vocal spouts are extremely discombobulating, littered with profanities and at times incoherent. 'Billy the loon, I am the loon', he says at one point, and it is hard to disagree; however, his closing segment is fascinatingly poetic and self-revealing, and the only piece of substance to take from 'Spaced'. 'I was born whole, fractured, divided, shattered into a billion fragments, a million-piece jigsaw with no this, and no that.'

Ever the eccentric writer, Corgan goes from a stark raving lunatic to Shakespeare or Wordsworth at the flick of a switch, bringing *Pisces Iscariot* to an end in the strangest of ways.

'Honeyspider II' (Corgan)
When the compilation was released in America, the first 2,000 vinyl pressings came with a bonus 7" containing 'Not Worth Asking'- the B-side on the Limited Potential 'I Am One' single, and 'Honeyspider II'.

Softer, cleaner and slower than the version which backed up 'Tristessa' on its 12" UK single, 'Honeyspider II' also shares fewer lyrics where Corgan repeatedly sings 'Didn't anyone say they knew I looked a lot like you, 'cause I do', in a relaxed and slightly hypnotic refrain. The original 'Honeyspider' is heavier set and tinged with new wave influence, its nucleus being the highly atmospheric guitar textures which shriek and shimmer. While the version heard on the bonus vinyl may be less emphatic, it is equally engaging.

Mellon Collie and the Infinite Sadness (1995)

Personnel:
Billy Corgan: lead vocals, guitar, piano, keyboard, autoharp
James Iha: guitar, lead vocals, backing vocals
D'arcy Wretzky: bass, lead vocals, backing vocals
Jimmy Chamberlin: drums, lead vocals
Recorded at: Pumpkinland, Chicago Recording Company, Chicago, Illinois, The
Village Recorder, Los Angeles, California (March-August 1995)
Produced by: Billy Corgan, Flood, Alan Moulder
Record label: Virgin
Release date: 24 October (UK), 25 October (US)
Chart positions: US: 1, UK: 4
Running time: 121:39

I went around saying I was inspired by Pink Floyd's *The Wall* to try to create
that kind of big, ambitious thing. And, of course, jerks in the media still take
me to task for saying that. For the record, from my point of view, I wasn't
trying to say that I had written my *Wall*... what I meant was that we were
trying to reach for something expansive like Pink Floyd achieved with *The
Wall,* as opposed to making a double album like *The White Album* by the
Beatles, which was basically a wider collection of great songs by a group.
Yes, those are crazy groups to ever compare yourself to, but as they say, you
have to aim high.
Billy Corgan

Before the *Siamese Dream* world tour had even drawn to a close, Billy Corgan
was already writing and demoing new material for the Pumpkins' next
album. *Siamese Dream* may have been the band's commercial breakthrough,
and a record that today is considered a rock classic, but in hindsight, it only
suggested at the greatness the quartet possessed.

Most artists would follow up a successful album with more of the same, but
repetition wasn't a word in Corgan's vocabulary. He was thinking bigger, with
no limitations; the impossible was possible. He was plotting a double album.
Enough material had been recorded to have turned *Siamese Dream* into a
double effort before being whittled down to thirteen tracks, but this time Corgan
was going all guns blazing to produce a generous and flamboyant offering very
rarely seen in mainstream music. Even Virgin Records was sceptical of the idea,
knowing that double albums didn't sell well, but despite the risk of commercial
failure, Corgan refused to bow down. Virgin even put forward the option of
releasing two separate discs like Guns N' Roses had in 1991. Both volumes of
Use Your Illusion were released on the same day and would go on to occupy
the *Billboard* 200's top two spots upon debut, collectively selling 1.5 million
copies in their first week on sale. Still, Corgan pushed for the double album, his
customary stubbornness eventually forcing Virgin to yield from their stance.

After a relatively short but profitable working relationship with Butch Vig, it was time for a change. The Pumpkins required being taken out of their comfort zone if such a resplendent vision was going to be brought to life, and so they turned to the British duo of Alan Moulder and Mark 'Flood' Ellis. Moulder had mixed *Siamese Dream,* so the band knew what he was capable of, while Flood had become an in-demand name in the production game. Getting his mainstream breakthrough when he was brought in to engineer U2's 1987 album, *The Joshua Tree*, Flood would actually withdraw from the gig to take up production duties on Erasure's sophomore release, *The Circus*. He had worked with the synth pop duo the year before, on their *Wonderland* debut, but *The Circus* was Erasure's coming of age, where four successful singles helped the record peak well inside the top ten of the UK Album Chart. Flood solidified his credentials further when he co-produced Nine Inch Nails' ground-breaking *Pretty Hate Machine* and *The Downward Spiral* LPs, the latter mixed by Moulder. And then, in 1995, The Smashing Pumpkins came calling.

Flood's first involvement was to send the group into a rehearsal space in a bid to capture the magic of their live performances. Nicknamed 'Pumpkinland' and located in an area of Chicago known for gang activity, the quartet recorded rough rhythm tracks and some of them were deemed good enough to go straight onto the album. Later, holing themselves up in the Chicago Recording Company studio, Corgan and Flood would work on vocals and song arrangements in one room while Moulder and the rest of the band did their bits in a second room. Corgan later revealed the intensity of the recording sessions, which finally moved over to Los Angeles' Village Recorder:

> A lot of *Mellon Collie* was tracked by the band at deafening volumes. I mean deafening. There was so much SPL (Sound Pressure Level) that it was physically uncomfortable. Your ears, your emotional resistance, would wear you down.

The approach to the album came with the mindset of it being the band's last, and it was a far more collaborative effort compared to how *Gish* and *Siamese Dream* had been put together. Corgan finally loosened his control, and even though he wrote almost all of the songs, Iha and Wretzky were allowed to record more of their guitar and bass parts. The album greatly benefitted from its organic and inclusive conception.

The title, *Mellon Collie and the Infinite Sadness*, had long been in Corgan's mind since thinking it up whilst walking around a dilapidated Coney Island in 1991. Its intentional misspelling followed on from that of 'Mayonaise', and by no means would it be the last time Corgan would use such a method. Based on 'The human condition of mortal sorrow' was how the band's leader described the twenty-eight-song opus, split into two halves with the sub-headings of *Dawn to Dusk*, and *Twilight to Starlight*; and at the same time, shunning the perception of *Mellon Collie...* being a concept album. '*The Wall* for Generation X', Corgan called it when speaking to the music press around release time, comparing it to Pink Floyd's sprawling 1979 rock opera, which spawned the classic songs 'Comfortably Numb', and 'Another Brick in the Wall'.

'Bullet with Butterfly Wings' was issued as the lead single a week ahead of the album's launch, a pulsating heavy rocker which found the Pumpkins picking up from where they left off on *Siamese Dream*; but the song didn't tell the full story of what was to come. Yes, there were other songs onboard containing the ear-splitting heaviness of previous material, but there were also songs to take the listener on fantastical adventures. There were even sultry ballads, swaying with a sparkling fragility, and all these ingredients had been thrown into a melting pot to cook up a prolific assortment of otherworldly delights. There is more than enough to appease the band's grunge and heavy metal followers, but the Chicagoans had expanded their repertoire by integrating new sounds and styles to break the mould of what a traditional rock band should be. *Mellon Collie and the Infinite Sadness* proved more than anything else that it was impossible to pigeonhole The Smashing Pumpkins.

Released in the UK on October 24 and a day later in America, the promotion for *Mellon Collie...* included a release party show held at Chicago's Riviera Theater, two days before the record hit US shelves. Broadcast across the country on FM radio, a handful of the new songs were performed alongside some choice cuts from *Siamese Dream*, and for a fun encore, the Pumpkins brought Cheap Trick onto the stage to play three of their classic tracks, 'Baby Loves to Rock', 'If You Want My Love', and 'Auf Wiedersehen'.

Mellon Collie... was lauded by critics, who rightfully called it the band's most ambitious and accomplished work. Any fears Virgin Records had of the double album being a failure were quickly dispelled when it roared to number 1 on the *Billboard* 200. It also topped the Australian, Canadian, Swedish and New Zealand album charts, and in the UK, the album equalled the result *Siamese Dream* achieved by peaking at 4. Within four months, the monumental *Mellon Collie and the Infinite Sadness* had been certified an incredible five times platinum in America, and today, it is one of approximately a hundred albums to ever be classified diamond, for selling in excess of ten million records.

Disc One – Dawn to Dusk
'Mellon Collie and the Infinite Sadness' (Corgan)
A new era of The Smashing Pumpkins begins in the most unsuspecting manner – with a three-minute piano piece acting as a rather affluent initiation. Billy Corgan constructed its arrangement on a 1920s-era piano he had bought and set up in his Wrigleyville home studio, a location he sardonically called 'Sadlands'.

The title track is undoubtedly a beautiful piece, a scene-setter of sorts that is entrenched in sadness, but occasionally its structure offers moments of hope. It has Corgan's blueprint all over without him ever having to say a single word. An earlier version simply titled 'Infinite Sadness' featured a full-band arrangement and played in a different key, but this instalment relies almost solely on the piano (the mellotron also makes a cameo) to transmit the tones which tug on the listener's heartstrings. Many have shed a tear to 'Mellon Collie and the Infinite Sadness', some have walked down the aisle to it on their wedding day, and some have even had the track played to remember a loved one at a funeral; such is the sentimental impact that this relatively simple piano arrangement has had on those who embraced its presence.

The Pumpkins begin album number three with something completely out of the ordinary, but it was quickly evident that the concoction of incoming songs was going to be bigger and bolder than anything the quartet had created before.

'Tonight, Tonight' (Corgan)

If there is one song on *Mellon Collie...* that can be attributed to turning alternative music on its head in the mid-nineties, then surely it is 'Tonight, Tonight', almost single-handedly shattering the glass ceiling for what could be incorporated into a rock song which had never been attempted, nor considered, before.

It is no surprise that 'Tonight, Tonight' has continually been named the Pumpkins' most aspiring song of their entire career, the basis of such statements revolving around the 30-piece string arrangement which governs direction from the first second to the last. Performed by the Chicago Symphony Orchestra, Billy Corgan described the recording experience as one of his most thrilling, and in the liner notes of the album's 2012 reissue, he hilariously reminisced:

> The string section itself was a harrowing affair; 30 foreigners on our rock and roll turf stuffed into the longwise expanse of two studio chambers. One noble scruff pulled me aside and said, 'Did you write this stuff? Reminds me of Mahler!'

The waves of glorious strings only have Jimmy Chamberlin's impassioned looping drum rolls to compete with, as the guitars and bass come in lower and lighter in the mix; very much a symphonic rock track, if you will. The theme of 'Tonight, Tonight' ultimately portrays hope and positivity, which Corgan proudly ignites on the everlasting and now classic lines of 'The impossible is possible tonight/believe in me as I believe in you, tonight', its moment coming during a final ascendency of the orchestra and some clinical Chamberlin drum rolls. It is a breathtaking crescendo.

By April 1996, *Mellon Collie and the Infinite Sadness* had already sold a whopping five million copies in the US alone, and when 'Tonight, Tonight' was released as the fourth single, it helped the record sell another five million, bringing in newer listeners who had never heard of The Smashing Pumpkins and became hooked on a rock song which sounded unlike any other. It became the band's highest-charting single in the UK by reaching number 7, gaining silver certification in the process for 200,000 copies sold, while in America, it hit the Mainstream Rock and Alternative Airplay charts at four and five, respectively. More acclaimed was the 36-peak position on the Hot 100, but as popular as the track was, its accompanying music video forged a legacy all of its own.

A handful of treatments were carefully considered before directors Jonathan Dayton and Valerie Faris offered their idea of a silent film-themed clip. The Pumpkins were making their record label a lot of money by now, so no expense appeared to be spared in creating a video just as sophisticated as its audio equivalent. Starring Tommy Kenny and Jill Talley, a husband-and-wife duo who were best known for being on the comedy sketch series *Mr. Show with Bob and David*, and who would go on to voice characters in everyone's favourite underwater cartoon, *SpongeBob SquarePants*, the video for 'Tonight, Tonight' was filmed with a turn of the century projector-style effect. Full of theatrical backdrops and puppetry, the plot follows Kenny and Talley flying off on a zeppelin balloon towards the moon, where when they arrive, they are attacked by some sinister-looking humanoid aliens. Fleeing captivity and leaving the moon on a rocket ship which crashes into the sea, the couple meets a merman resembling the sea god Poseidon, who treats his guests to an underwater entertainment show performed by a mermaid, starfishes and an octopus. When the protagonists eventually return to the surface, they are saved by a passing steamboat with the name S.S. Mélies, referring to the French illusionist and film director whose 1902 short film, *A Trip to the Moon*, provided the main inspiration for this stunning music video.

The band members also get into character here, dressing in turn-of-the-century clothing and playing old acoustic instruments such as a harp guitar, and what was reported to be a 1924 Gibson Mando bass. Even before filming had begun the video ran into difficulties, when props and costumes proved hard to come by in and around Los Angeles. At the same time, James Cameron had started filming his epic *Titanic* movie, and if you've seen it, you'll know he needed a lot of period gear to bring those scenes to life. At risk of having to cancel the video shoot and consider another treatment, Dayton and Faris managed to rent anything that was made available to them before hiring special designers who could remake the costumes into something more suitable for the era and style they had been planned for.

The video was nominated for EIGHT awards at the 1996 *MTV* VMAs, winning six of them in the categories of Video of the Year, Breakthrough Video, Best Direction in a Video, Best Special Effects in a Video, Best Art

Direction in a Video and Best Cinematography in a Video. In 1997, 'Tonight, Tonight' was nominated in the Best Music Video, Short Form GRAMMY category, but it lost out to the Beatles 'Free as a Bird', first written by John Lennon in 1977 but released in 1995 to promote a new video documentary and compilation album.

'Tonight, Tonight' is one of the Pumpkins' most enduring songs and has been played live over 900 times. It remains as fascinating and fresh today as it did upon first listen all those years ago, and it showed that alternative rock wasn't just about heavy guitars, deep throbbing bass lines and fiery drum patterns. A timeless classic.

'Jellybelly' (Corgan)

After the early optimism offered by the opening two tracks, 'Jellybelly' turns the air sour with a ferociously metallic intro built around swirling guitars and a drum sequence of malevolent proportions. In complete contrast to 'Tonight, Tonight', Billy Corgan shifts his focus to the negative aspects of the human condition, where the opening line of 'Welcome to nowhere fast, nothing here ever lasts' finds its writer back in his depressive comfort zone.

'Jellybelly' is one of the heaviest songs on the album, but it is also one of the best, and it was no coincidence that the track should be found so high up the tracklisting. 'Living makes me sick, so sick I wish I'd die' continues Corgan, incidentally one of his favourite lyrics, but despite the breakneck drive which pulses throughout, its chorus is rather melodic and catchy in distinction. Corgan actually wanted 'Jellybelly' to be the lead single, but on this occasion, he didn't get his way. Instead, it stands as a convincing album track and regardless of all the newer elements the band would present over the next hour or so, 'Jellybelly' confirmed the Pumpkins were still happy to churn out some straightforward and rousing rockers when they felt like it.

'Zero' (Corgan)

The first track recorded for *Mellon Collie...* and possessing one of the Pumpkins' most famous lead riffs, 'Zero' is another heavy number but not so as asphyxiating as 'Jellybelly' before it.

The band considered 'Zero' as 'cybermetal', and James Iha even felt its sound reminded him of something that British heavy metal masters Judas Priest would come up with, and while that may be hard to agree with, this short and sharp stab certainly benefits from the screeching guitars and the fuzz and distortion which envelops the latterly short-tempered solo.

Corgan wrote 'Zero' as a response to those who considered him a rock god and his reluctance to assume such an elevated position. The song offers multiple lines of memorable substance, none the more so than the repelling sequence of 'Emptiness is loneliness, and loneliness is cleanliness, and cleanliness is godliness, and God is empty, just like me.' The lyrics are brilliantly comprised throughout, so much so that Corgan was always going to come out of the song with more hero worship than he previously had. It most certainly wasn't his intention, but fronting one of the biggest rock bands in the world was always going to come with a price to pay.

Instead of releasing 'Zero' as a standard single, the song headlined a seven-track EP totalling more than 40 minutes in length. The B-sides will be discussed in due course. By the time it was released in April 1996, Corgan's marriage to Chris Fabian had ended and he was now dating Ukrainian photographer and video director Yelena Yemchuk, and she came in to direct the 'Zero' video. *NME* described it as 'cinematic and creepy', set in a Roman-style mansion where the Pumpkins perform 'Zero' for a roomful of guests who are dressed in period outfits. The band themselves are largely dressed in black, and their then-touring keyboard player, Jonathan Melvoin, can be seen playing whilst wearing a grey suit.

'Zero' charted on the *Billboard* 200, as EPs were not considered as singles, but still, it reached 46 and went gold after shifting 500,000 copies. The smash hit cartoon *The Simpsons* regularly featured guest spots by rock bands during its episodes throughout the 1990s. Korn, Metallica, R.E.M. and U2 were just a small handful of acts to have starred in the show, and in episode 24 of the seventh season (*Homerpalooza*), The Smashing Pumpkins made a cameo appearance and performed a section of 'Zero' to further boost its promotion.

Corgan soon embraced an alter ego known as 'Zero', and, at the same time, created a t-shirt with the word printed on the front and with a star underneath it. The shirt has since become an iconic piece of merchandise that many a fan has owned and worn with pride.

'Here Is No Why' (Corgan)

The origins of 'Here Is No Why' date back to the summer of 1994, when the song was played live for the one and only time by Corgan's on-off side-project, Starchildren. Formed in 1990, the band had varying members who, at one point or another, included Jimmy Chamberlin and Kerry Brown in its line-up; however, Starchildren only released two official songs during their existence- 'Delusions of Candor' on a split 7" with fellow Chicago rock act Catherine, and a cover of Joy Division's 'Isolation' on a tribute album to the British post-punks, titled *A Means to an End: The Music of Joy Division*.

First titled 'Just Between', the version of 'Here Is No Why' the world came to know is a mid-tempo alt rock anthem with driving guitars and a soaring chorus, full of overly dramatic but vivid lyricism, which Corgan admitted were self-absorbed and harked back to his younger years:

The useless drag of another day,
The endless drags of a death rock boy,
Mascara sure and lipstick lost,
Glitter burned by restless thoughts of being forgotten.

59

Musically, 'Here Is No Why' has one of the strongest compositions on *Mellon Collie...*, from the rhythmic verses where the cleaner guitars sound off in a stop-start motion to its radio-friendly hook that is impossible to not sing along to. It could have easily been a single contender, but instead, it stands tall as a sublime album track.

'Bullet with Butterfly Wings' (Corgan)

'The world is a vampire,' sings Corgan during the opening foray of 'Bullet with Butterfly Wings' – perhaps the most famous The Smashing Pumpkins song of them all.

As previously mentioned, Corgan wanted to release 'Jellybelly' as the lead single, rebelling against the mainstream by putting out an exceedingly abrasive song which he knew would perhaps be a little too much for some to digest. On this occasion, he was outvoted, though, because everyone else could see the potential 'Bullet with Butterfly Wings' had. From its tension-strained lead riff and rhythm section, to the arena-sized chorus where Corgan contests fame once again in the scorching line of 'Despite all my rage, I am still just a rat in a cage'; there was no getting away from one of the album's most overbearing themes.

The song first came to be while the Pumpkins were recording for the *BBC*, during the same session where they laid down 'Landslide'. In the *Mellon Collie...* liner notes, Corgan extended:

I was sitting there bored out of my mind, (the producers) were dicking around with some microphone, and I had this line in my head, 'Despite all my rage, I'm still just a rat in a cage'. I was just sitting there bored, and I picked up the guitar, and I started singing. But, what if the guy had been like, 'Ooh, we're ready!?' People don't appreciate that there's a thing that needs to happen. The stars need to align.

'Bullet with Butterfly Wings' is peak The Smashing Pumpkins. It contains everything the quartet had already mastered, and then they turned the dial up to eleven. The riffs, the bass, Chamberlin's powerhouse drumming; angst, melody, and distortion. The band had every base covered.

Released on October 16 – a week before *Mellon Collie...* – the single lit up radio and secured the Pumpkins' first Top 40 hit on the Hot 100, reaching 22. It also spent six weeks at two on the Modern Rock Tracks chart, while in the UK, it peaked at 20.

Having worked with The Offspring, Hole, Blind Melon, Nirvana and a whole other host of established rock acts, Samuel Bayer was recruited to direct a music video where the Pumpkins debuted a glam look; and slightly gothic too. It would be the last time people would see Billy Corgan with hair, as by the time the video was released, he had already gone bald, but here he had dyed black hair and is wearing shiny silver trousers. He also has his

'Zero' shirt on. D'arcy is wearing a fancy wedding-like dress, and James can be seen in a swanky suit. The subplot features a load of goldmine workers who, while taking a break, watch the Pumpkins perform. At one point, a load of them begin fighting before rain begins to fall and the workers bathe themselves clean.

'Bullet with Butterfly Wings' was certified silver in the UK and gold in America. In 1997, the song won a GRAMMY in the Best Hard Rock Performance category, beating Alice in Chains, Rage Against the Machine, Soundgarden and Stone Temple Pilots. After the 9/11 terrorist attacks, 'Bullet' was listed as one of 165 songs which Clear Channel Communications (now known as iHeartMedia) recommended should be withdrawn from US radio. Fingering those with titles or lyrics which could have been interpreted as either referring to the atrocities or inciting retaliation, this was the only Pumpkins song to be pulled into question. Rage Against the Machine, however, found their entire discography included in the manifesto.

Expectedly, one of the most played songs in the live environment, 'Bullet with Butterfly Wings' has also been covered by multiple rock acts in the years since its release. Latin metallers Ill Niňo, melodic hardcore outfit Four Year Strong, even Sigue Sigue Sputnik have chosen to take on the track- not that the original could ever be bettered. When later recounting his time working on *Mellon Collie...*, Flood spoke of the immediate impact of 'Bullet with Butterfly Wings':

With 'Bullet', really early on when we were going through all the demos, it was quite obvious that the great thing about working with the Pumpkins was that it was obvious which tracks were going to be the real main players. That was most definitely one of them, and we all knew it because it had the energy we wanted to capture.

'To Forgive' (Corgan)

As its title suggests, 'To Forgive' finds Corgan finally ready to let go of his childhood trauma, with lyrics of anguish and depression relayed over sombre and downbeat instrumentation. D'arcy's bass has an exaggerated voice here, playing nicely with the delicate semi-acoustic guitar tones and stoic drum pattern.

'I sensed my loss before I even learned to talk', sings Corgan, 'and I remember my birthdays, empty party afternoons won't come back', he continues as he engages with the listener as if begging for acceptance from whoever is willing to offer it. 'To Forgive' separates itself from most of the *Mellon Collie...* tracklisting in that it does not rely on those multi-layered guitars more commonly used elsewhere. It is raw in its presentation and what you hear is what you get, while Iha's use of an E-bow creates the subtle synth-like sounds that come in halfway through. Another excellent song.

'Fuck You (An Ode to No One)' (Corgan)

'The basic thing is fuck everybody,' said Corgan when asked about the meaning behind a song that shows his frustration with life and everything in it, the repeated use of the word 'disconnect' perfectly underlining his desire to shut out the whole world if it means he can find some internal peace.

It was only on later issues of the album that the 'Fuck You' part was added to the title, the Über-heavy song opening with a scratchy riff not too dissimilar to the intro of KISS' 'I Was Made For Lovin' You', except this is immediately more aggressive in tone. Corgan has increased verve in his vocals here, a swagger that becomes louder as the track progresses, and the music follows suit. High in tempo, fractious and delightfully unbalanced, the razor-sharp riffing and cerebral drum blasts paint a bleak picture of the disgust the songwriter is feeling. The volatile guitar solo is tumultuous, to say the least, where Corgan gets the desired outcome by standing right next to his purposely overloud amp. Battling to play harder in order to overthrow the feedback, Corgan played until his fingers bled, the result being another highly charged solo exuding plenty of energy and emotion.

As part of the tyrannical schedule that producer Flood set out for the band, 'Fuck You' was often rehearsed two or three times a day before it was finally recorded; however, its early arrangements were actually put together by Corgan and Alan Moulder, the first time the two had worked together while Flood took some time away from the studio. 'I disconnect the act, I disconnect the dots, I disconnect the me in me' sings Corgan with his fierce snarl, his lyrics at times just as explosive as the vitriolic instrumentation. A fan favourite for anyone who at some point in their lives, has felt like screaming, 'Fuck you all and fuck everything'. Don't pretend you're not one of those people.

'Love' (Corgan)

Super fuzzy but brilliantly switching the flow once more, 'Love' is a dense rocker which presents its theme as being harsh and cruel instead of positively affectionate. A flanger pedal is used on the guitar, where the delays cause a sweeping effect to make everything sound that little bit heavier and intense, as does the distortion effect on Corgan's vocals to create further nihilism. At this time, the singer's marriage to Chris Fabian was all but over, and so his conscious attack on love in the romantic sense was always going to be antagonistic. 'When I lost my mind, I knew I was in for a long night' he howls, which leads into a reverberant guitar solo where its pitch and tone are extremely bleak. 'Love' is an interesting addition to *Mellon Collie...* and it enters another new area for the Pumpkins to investigate. Nine tracks in and the album is already overdosing on killer cuts.

'Cupid de Locke' (Corgan)

'To counter-balance our many dark excursions into the void, I sought some refuge by writing whimsically as well...' wrote Corgan in the *Mellon Collie...*

reissue liner notes, when discussing a track which is a far departure from anything the Pumpkins had ever done in their career up to this point.

'Cupid de Locke' is a beautifully intricate but experimental affair where the band incorporate household items to use as percussion. Saltshakers (believed to actually be bottles of aspirin) and pairs of scissors formulate the subtle 'beats'; however, they play second fiddle to some glittery harp arpeggios as Corgan challenges himself to expand his creative loins outside of the rock and roll scope.

The song's title stems from the 17th-century composer Matthew Locke, who scored a play which was performed in courtyards around England under the name of *Cupid and Death*. In traditional Billy Corgan keeping, he accompanies the lush and atmospheric music with lyrics shrouded in doom and gloom, summed up perfectly in this closing Shakespearean passage:

We seek the unseekable and we speak the unspeakable,
Our hopes dead gathering dust to dust,
In faith, in compassion, and in love.

Nicely placed in the tracklisting to offer a period of calm after the lethal doses of 'Fuck You...' and 'Love', 'Cupid de Locke' is a glistening interlude that, even with the multifarious acts seen thus far, no one could have possibly predicted to have come from the Pumpkins.

'Galapogos' (Corgan)

With another intentionally misspelt title, 'Galapogos' is indeed in reference to the Galàpagos Islands, where Charles Darwin studied, observed, and collected the research which would later contribute to this theory of evolution. Relating the isolation of the islands to that of his failing marriage, Corgan writes an erstwhile love letter with a naïve innocence, hoping his relationship could possibly survive through life's trials and tribulations.

This light and unthreatening song very much settles into its mid-album position, never really getting out of second gear, even though it is clearly carefully crafted and multi-layered. 'I won't deny the pain, I won't deny the change, and should I fall from grace here with you, will you leave me too?' sings Corgan with an element of fear in his fragile tones, painting a picture of vulnerability and emphasising the importance of how two people must form an emotional connection to be able to provide support for one another.

'Muzzle' (Corgan)

One of the last songs written for *Mellon Collie...*, 'Muzzle' is an anthemic number containing all the traits of a classic The Smashing Pumpkins radio rocker. Documenting what Corgan felt the public's perception of him was, the singer provides an enterprising attack on music critics who he wondered may be getting tired of hearing the same angst-ridden themes running through his songs. 'The idea of a muzzle refers to thinking my life would be far simpler if I just kept my trap shut', he said, perhaps beginning to reap what he was sowing.

Despite his mindset, 'Muzzle' is rather upbeat, the distorted guitars are rather breezy as Chamberlin's drumming expresses an emotion that replaces his usual reliance on technicality. 'My life has been extraordinary, blessed and cursed and won', sings Corgan as he takes stock of his present standing as one of rock's most popular frontmen – clearly, the morbid depression he often writes with was working wonders for him.

Released as a promotional single in August 1996, 'Muzzle' hit eight on Alternative Airplay and ten on Mainstream Rock Tracks, the song helping continue *Mellon Collie's* second mainstream wind, which had kickstarted on the back of the 'Tonight, Tonight' single. Regardless of how Corgan thought people saw him, rock fans all over could not get enough of him and his band of musical superheroes, and at this point, the album had gone seven times platinum in the US of A.

'Porcelina of the Vast Oceans' (Corgan)
Following in the footsteps of 'Silverfuck' and 'Starla', here is another long and winding opus that clocks in at 9:21. Sections of 'Porcelina of the Vast Oceans' were recorded at different times, using various instruments and setups which, once completed, were thrown into Pro Tools. The result is this glamorous tour de force with its loose concept of the character Porcelina, who calls the song's narrator towards a realm of peace and tranquillity. The lyrics are made up of lines of disjointed poetry found in some of Corgan's old notebooks, of which he commented as being 'vague allusions to mythic tides and sinking ships seemed only to enhance the unconscious feeling within'.

From the slow-building psychy intro with its twirling guitars and swish cymbal rides, to the harder portion made up of thick, distortion-induced guitars and lively drum patterns, 'Porcelina' further showcases Billy Corgan's songwriting development since the *Siamese Dream* days. His and James Iha's guitars mesh well in the heavier moments; listening to the song with a good set of headphones accentuates this point clearer. There is no denying the importance of the ethereal sounds and effects which announce themselves during the final flourish, hovering around some penetrating feedback on what quickly becomes a spine-tingling outro. 'Porcelina of the Vast Oceans' is another mesmerising long-player that never outstays its welcome; a captivating and absorbing listen where you cannot help but give the song your undivided attention.

'Take Me Down' (Iha)
One of only two tracks on the double album to be solely credited to James Iha, 'Take Me Down' would end up causing the guitarist to forfeit his songwriting talents in the band in the future.

Above: Future rock superstars. (*Virgin*)

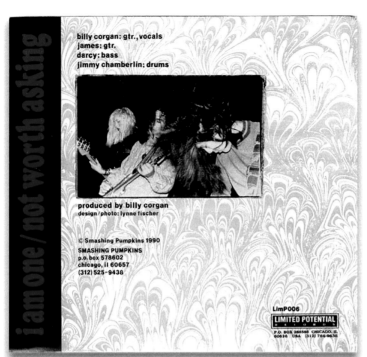

Left: The first single to be unleashed on an unsuspecting world: 'I Am One'. (*Limited Potential*)

Right: The Pumpkins' only release on the legendary Sub Pop label: 'Tristessa'. (*Sub Pop*)

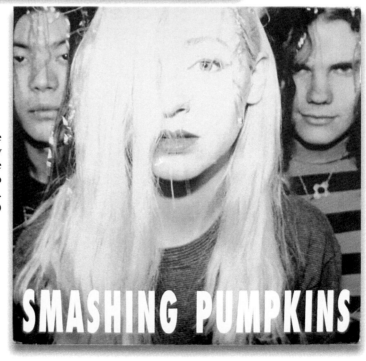

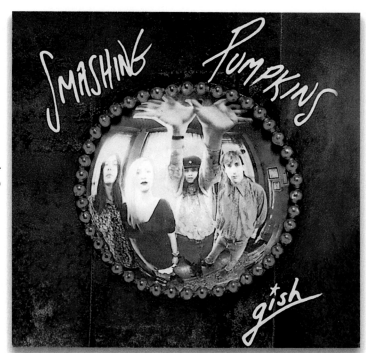

Right: *Gish* cover art. (*Caroline*)

Left: The album that changed everything: *Siamese Dream*. (*Virgin*)

Left: Cover art for the 'Today' single. (*Virgin*)

Right: A still from the colourful 'Today' music video.

Left: Billy Corgan – all out of ice cream... and paint.

Right: The *Heart* cover art for the 'Disarm' single. (*Virgin*)

Left: Billy 'shouting' from the rooftops in the 'Disarm' music video.

Right: D'arcy didn't suffer from vertigo. Also from the 'Disarm' music video.

Left: A B-sides album better than most bands' A-side material: *Pisces Iscariot*. (*Virgin*)

Right: *Earphoria* live album cover art. (*Virgin*)

Left: Bullet with Butterfly Wings': the Pumpkins' next rousing single. (*Virgin*)

Right: In the 'Bullet…' music video, Billy first revealed the now-legendary 'Zero' t-shirt.

Left: In an explosive 1990s rock scene, the Pumpkins were never ones to shy away from showing their teeth.

Right: James Iha – his rhythmic guitars sent many listeners into a dreamlike state.

Left: Up there with the greatest ever double albums: *Mellon Collie and the Infinite Sadness.* (*Virgin*)

Right: Treading new waters for the band, '1979' became an unexpected mainstream hit. (*Virgin*)

Billboard 200
WEEK OF NOVEMBER 11, 1995

THIS WEEK	AWARD ⓘ	LAST WEEK	PEAK POS.	WKS ON CHART
1 NEW **Mellon Collie And The Infinite ..** The Smashing Pumpkins				
(★)	-	1	1	+
2 ↓ **Daydream** Mariah Carey				
	1	1	4	+
3 ↓ **Jagged Little Pill** Alanis Morissette				
	2	1	20	+
4 NEW **Ozzmosis** Ozzy Osbourne				
★	-	4	1	+
5 NEW **The Greatest Hits Collection** Alan Jackson				
★	-	5	1	+

Left: The *Billboard* 200 Top Five on 11 November 1995. (*Billboard.com*)

Right: The Pumpkins' most elaborate and artistic music video: 'Tonight, Tonight'.

Left: The impossible was indeed possible.

Right: Even as sea creatures, the Pumpkins put on one hell of a show.

Above: The Chicago Four. (*Virgin*)

Below: Set to go global. (*Virgin*)

Right: 'Thirty-Three' single cover art. (*Virgin*)

Left: The *Aeroplane Flies High* Boxset: more B-side delights. (*Virgin*)

Left: A new electronic era of the Pumpkins arrived in the form of *Adore*. (*Virgin*)

Right: Another captivating music video, 'Ava Adore' was filmed in one long take.

Left: Billy 'Uncle Fester' Corgan: powering through despite almost giving up on the 'Ava Adore' video shoot.

Right: Jimmy Chamberlin returned for *Machina/The Machines of God*, as did those crunching guitars. (*Virgin*)

The Everlasting Gaze (4:01)

THE SMASHING PUMPKINS
'The Everlasting Gaze'
New single from the new album
'MACHINA...machines of God'
ALBUM OUT FEB 28.

Left: 'The Everlasting Gaze' promotional single release. (*Virgin*)

Above: A quick video shoot for 'The Everlasting Gaze' while in London, England.

Below: Green with envy.

Right: The classic line-up's final album, bowing out in style with the blistering *Machina II/The Friends & Enemies of Modern Music*. (*Constantinople*)

Left: The Pumpkins' 'final' show at the Metro on 2 December 2000. (*Metro Chicago*)

Left: Three up-and-coming bands who went on to sell over 250 million records between them.

Right: One of many eye-catching posters released for shows on the *Mellon Collie...* tour.

Not a million miles away from 'Blew Away' on the *Pisces Iscariot* compilation, this is also a love-themed acoustic plod which is Beatles-esque and wholly sweet and innocent. Iha's soft and shy vocals fail to set the world on fire; in fact, everything about 'Take Me Down', which also features guest musician Greg Leisz playing the pedal and lap steel guitar overdubs, is so far apart from what the rest of *Mellon Collie...* has to offer. In the reissue liner notes, Corgan admitted to wanting to include the song from the beginning, but he couldn't see where it would fit it in. In the end, he decided to relegate Iha's baby to the final track on the *Dawn to Dusk* disc, which in turn upset its writer. From that moment, Iha decided not to contribute to future Pumpkins songs, such was his dismay at the lack of faith shown in his work.

'Take Me Down' is a 'nice' song, and that is perhaps the best way to describe it. It certainly does feel out of place, sticking out like a sore thumb in comparison to 'Tonight, Tonight', 'Bullet with Butterfly Wings', 'Love', and basically every other track on the first disc. It wouldn't have been out of character for Corgan to drop the song completely if he really wanted to, so at least it is here to appease Iha, even if it acts as a kind of afterthought.

Disc Two – Twilight to Starlight
'Where Boys Fear to Tread' (Corgan)
Opening the second disc, 'Where Boys Fear to Tread' is a rather metallic and grunge-tinged song in which the Pumpkins performed for the very first time while the tape was rolling, and this is the result.

It's an interesting way to record a song, its instantly live presentation harnessing a rawness that the rest of the *Mellon Collie...* tracks didn't have due to their generally richer mixes. The low-fi sound of the guitar comes from Corgan's 1974 *Fender* Stratocaster, also used on the main rhythm of 'Muzzle' and on 'Bullet for Butterfly Wings'. At various points, a rocket launcher sample is audible, taken from the *Doom* video game – a correlation coming from a running joke between the band and the game's creators since December 1993 (Google 'SPISPOPD' to find out more). Corgan orchestrates the changes in the song, guiding the rest of the band and saluting when the right moment comes to switch things up, and the abrupt, cut-off ending you hear is down to Jimmy Chamberlin, who continued playing on after the planned final note.

As she did when talking about certain songs from *Siamese Dream,* Courtney Love was back in full-on vanity mode when she declared 'Where Boys Fear to Tread' had been written about her brief relationship with Nine Inch Nails' head honcho, Trent Reznor, of which Billy Corgan reportedly disapproved. It is worth mentioning here that Love and Reznor's meeting came after the death of Kurt Cobain, and while Corgan was on and off the scene for many years, it is hard to say if the Pumpkin was more than just a friend at this point towards the end of 1994. Nevertheless, the lyrical content of this song in no way appears to venture towards Love, and the words are very much left open to interpretation, whilst more than content to settle into ambiguity.

'Bodies' (Corgan)

'Bodies' continues the second side's blistering start by pushing the rawness of 'Where Boys Fear to Tread' even farther. This is The Smashing Pumpkins in inspired form, the guitars firing up from the opening gargle of fiery feedback to supply some angsty power chords, which, along with Chamberlin's machine gun drumming, drive this powerful number.

Corgan delivers one of his most potent vocal performances, using all of his styles and tones at one point or another, his most unruly moment coming on the repeated uttering of his now famous and gritty line of 'love is suicide'. The lyric does not need any deciphering, and Corgan's increasing screams and snarls could not be more emotionally retorted if he tried.

'Bodies' may have one of the more simplistic arrangements, but sometimes less is very much more. It nicely captures the band's ability of retaining a catchiness to songs clearly focused on and around anger and resentment, and this certified crowd-pleaser appears out of nowhere to slay and lay waste. When talking about 'Bodies' in later years, Corgan admitted that the recording process was an intense and agitated affair, but it clearly helped elevate the song to heights it may not have been able to reach otherwise:

Once we moved from Pumpkinland to the sterile drawl of the Chicago Recording Company, we still had some tracks to cut. For 'Bodies', our producer Flood loaded in a full P.A. and cranked the subs so hard that in the sealed room, we were nauseous with the pressure being thrown about. Naturally, we became agitated and uncomfortable, which in turn meant our work with one another became terse.

'Thirty-Three' (Corgan)

As with the upcoming '1979', 'Thirty-Three' hints at where The Smashing Pumpkins would go in the future with their musical style, stripping back on guitar-driven rock in favour of experimentation, with a heavier emphasis on electronics.

'Thirty-Three' was actually the first song completed for *Mellon Collie...*, telling the story of 'the death of youth and innocence' as Billy Corgan described it. It seems he is at a point where he is already regretting his career path, longing for the return of the privacy he once had, which evaporated the second his band hit lift-off. 'And for a moment I lose myself, wrapped up in the pleasures of the world', he sings on this country-tinged, slightly shoegaze track, which features a delightful piano melody and multiple slide guitars. Corgan used a vocoder to generate the string sounds that gyrate in the background, while the drum machine track running through a flanger was from the actual demo recording because Corgan could not remember how to re-create it later on.

'Deep in thought I forgive everyone, as the cluttered streets greet me once again,' the frontman later adds, the line self-explanatory as his new life brings him crashing back down to earth and highlights the vulnerability he feels when all are eyes are firmly transfixed on him. The musical arrangement remains compelling, though, because, upon its first arrival, it provided an unusual swerve from the band. When you have a songwriter who is willing to leave no stone unturned, however, perhaps there should be no surprise, and the album's genre-bending credibility increases just as its soundscape expands.

Chosen as the fifth and ultimately final single from *Mellon Collie...*, 'Thirty-Three' was released on 11 November 1996. As seen in the song's music video, which was again directed by Yelena Yemchuk but with more involvement from Corgan, The Smashing Pumpkins were now a three-piece band.

Jonathan Melvoin had joined the Pumpkins towards the end of 1995, when the band required help in obtaining a fuller sound whilst performing their *Mellon Collie* cuts live. Melvoin came with a rich musical background. His father had played piano on the Beach Boys' *Pet Sounds* album, and he had also recorded with Frank Sinatra, John Lennon and Tom Waits. Jonathan's sister, Wendy, had been part of Prince's band, The Revolution, playing guitar on songs which would star on the *Purple Rain* and *Around the World in a Day* albums. Jonathan and his other sister, Susannah, had also contributed to some of Prince's work, including his side project with The Family. He was also a talented drummer, having first picked up a set of sticks around the age of five and going on to play in a handful of punk rock bands – most notably The Dickies.

Sadly, Melvoin was dabbling with heroin by 1995, even though upon being unveiled as the Pumpkins' touring keyboardist, he was quoted as saying how proud he was that the quartet was a 'drug-free band'. On the evening before the Pumpkins were due to play New York City's Madison Square Garden for the very first time, Jimmy Chamberlin had scored a bag of heroin with the street name 'Red Rum'. A stint in rehab upon the completion of *Siamese Dream* had failed to cure the drummer's addictions, and he was continuing to use well into 1996. A particularly potent form of heroin and up to 80% pure, such a product was intended to be snorted rather than injected, but likely unaware, Chamberlin and Melvoin did indeed inject the drug in their Regency Hotel rooms in Park Avenue. Both men passed out, and only Chamberlin woke up again. In the early hours of 12 June 1996, Jonathan Melvoin was declared dead, his toxicology report confirming his death by a combination of heroin and alcohol. Chamberlin was later charged with misdemeanour possession of a controlled substance. Because Melvoin was already dead when Chamberlin came around, the drummer wasn't faced with any negligence charges as tests proved any quicker action and 911 calls would not have changed the outcome. Sadly, 'Red Rum' gained in popularity due to the publicity surrounding the overdoses of two musicians from one of the world's biggest rock bands. In the aftermath of the events, Chamberlin was fired from The Smashing Pumpkins. He was later replaced by Matt Walker from the industrial rock band Filter, whose 1995 debut album, *Short Bus*, went platinum in America on the back of the hit single, 'Hey Man Nice Shot'. For the rest of the tour, Jimmy Flemion from Milwaukee's The Frogs was brought in to play the keys.

In an intentional departure from previous music videos, 'Thirty-Three' includes images directly relating to lines in the song. Filmed in a stop-motion technique, the video remained artistic with the use of fancy costumes, film sets, and carefully constructed scenes. Seeing a Chamberlin-less Pumpkins was certainly strange at the time.

'Thirty-Three' reached 39 on the Hot 100, 2 on Alternative Airplay, and 18 on Mainstream Rock Tracks. In the UK, the song scored a decent 21. A massive stylistic departure for the Pumpkins, 'Thirty-Three' has gone on to be one of the band's most popular songs. Corgan's beautifully imaginative lyrics are compelling, and his elevated line of 'You can make it last forever' provides the emotional key that unlocked many a listener into taking the song to their hearts.

'In the Arms of Sleep' (Corgan)

Neo psychedelic? Folk? Gothic? 'In the Arms of Sleep' could be considered any or all of these at one point or another. A mostly acoustic but certainly haunting ballad in which Corgan openly admits to his craving for constant love and affection, the second disc of the album seems to have the more direct songs covering his failed marriage.

His vocals are pained and line after line is filled with despair, but the stunning melodies which counteract the song's mood are what makes this song so special. 'I'll always need her more than she could ever need me,' sings Corgan, causing a lump in the throat, while the closing protestation of 'Suffer my desire' is another of the album's most profound lines.

While 'In the Arms of Sleep' may be an acoustic lullaby, it is still a rich and full presentation through its layered production. It is absorbing, a song which is just as enjoyable after each repeated listen, and you could even go so far as to say that it could be one of the band's most underrated tracks.

'1979' (Corgan)

1984 was the year Billy Corgan considered he transitioned into adolescence, discussed during a 2022 episode of his *Thirty-Three* podcast and at the same time, putting a slight dampener on the meaning behind one of his greatest-ever songs.

Instead, the title '1979' stems from a poem, which, like the song, surrounds a random year, but it does have a nice ring to it. When released as the follow-up single to 'Bullet with Butterfly Wings', '1979' offered the first insight into a new direction for the quartet, toying with manipulated and looped electronic samples; the results producing a rather dizzying spectacle. The repetitive vocal loop that lasts the course can at first seem annoying; however, '1979' became an instant and unexpected hit. Corgan was reluctant to release the song as a single, but Virgin saw the potential of its crossover ability. It didn't happen often, but in this case, Virgin got their way.

'1979' was not an easy song to bring to fruition, as Corgan explained in the *Mellon Collie...* liner notes:

> Every time we tried to play it as a band, it sounded like the Rolling Stones – and not in a good way. It came out too bluesy. We were running out of time and packing up for LA. Finally, Flood said, 'What's going on with this song? Tomorrow is D-day, we either finish this song or it's off the record.' So I went home that night, finished all the lyrics, did a demo that sounds remarkably like the final record. I came in the next day with the demo, and Flood said, 'I love it. Now make it happen.' We went in the room and cut it in one day.

Considered his most personally important song on the entire album, Corgan's excellently compiled but non-specific lyrics tell of teenage innocence and boredom with adulthood on the horizon; of which listeners in the Pumpkins' chosen demographic were able to relate to.

Jonathan Dayton and Valerie Faris returned to direct the music video, with a concept devised by Corgan portraying an idealised version of what teenage life could be like. A group of suburban teens spend the first half driving around in a 1972 Dodge Charger, having carefree fun and harming no one. The later party scene in which the Pumpkins perform for a house full of teens is colourful and light-hearted; however, it had to be re-filmed when the original tapes were left on the roof of a car and later destroyed. At the 1996 VMA's, '1979' won Best Alternative Video.

The single was released in late January of 1996, and it became the Pumpkins' highest-charting Hot 100 song when it peaked at 12. '1979' also reached number 1 on both the Alternative Airplay and Mainstream Rock Tracks charts and in the UK, it hit number 16. The song also earned two nods at the 1997 GRAMMY Awards; however, it lost out to Eric Clapton in the Record of the Year category, and the Dave Matthews Band in the Best Rock Performance field.

'1979' has aged gracefully, its experimental nature coming across pure and its pop hooks proving irresistible. It is a chilled-out alternative rock song which doesn't rely on heavy instrumentation to make its impact, in fact, '90s alt rock had never sounded so poignant and reflective. Many streaming service playlists tend to include '1979' to best represent The Smashing Pumpkins' contribution towards defining the decade, and in some ways, the song is arguably more important today, if not at least appropriate to these times of uncertainty in which we live.

There is a certain romanticism to the fact that this was the last song recorded for *Mellon Collie...*, completed at the eleventh hour and with barely any more time to spare, and the gargantuan impact '1979' had on the rock

---

world was epitomised by the fact that everything Corgan seemed to touch ended up turning to gold.

'Tales of a Scorched Earth' (Corgan)
Luring listeners into a false sense of security with the 'Thirty-Three', 'In the Arms of Sleep' and '1979' triple-header, the Pumpkins come out fighting on the ferocious 'Tales of a Scorched Earth'.

This is full-on heavy metal, with layers of distorted guitar overdubs and Billy Corgan in psychotic form with his vocals. There is a harsh effect to them, which only adds to the tension, as hostile lyrical passages reveal his teenage nihilism mindset. 'Farewell, goodnight, last one out, turn out the lights, and let me be, let me die inside,' he screeches early on; the mood immediately darkened in favour of the Yin over the Yang. Jimmy Chamberlin's double-kick drum salvos are effortless, while the laser-like feedback coming from the Corgan/Iha tag team fight one another for the right of top dog. D'arcy's bass struggles for prominence, but her deep tones do stake a claim here and there.

'Why do the same old things keep happening, because beyond my hopes there are no feelings?' continues a depressive Corgan, both lyrics and instrumentation completely overwhelming the listener, as they are constantly being pulled one way and then the other by the album's persistent re-direction.

The vocal recording for this rampant album track was completed in just two takes, and Corgan later admitted he was unable to sing it live. The one and only time he did attempt it was during the band's rescheduled Madison Square Garden concert on 17 September, some two months after Jonathan Melvoin's death and Jimmy Chamberlin's resultant firing. If you happened to be at that concert in MSG, you witnessed a bit of history hearing 'Tales of a Scorched Earth', and if this song doesn't blow off the cobwebs, then no other Pumpkins track will.

'Thru the Eyes of Ruby' (Corgan)
Throwing in a bit of prog rock, 'Thru the Eyes of Ruby' is another seven-plus minute composition which regularly shifts in dynamics, and it quickly became many a fan's favourite song on *Mellon Collie....*

Corgan's failing marriage provides the lyrical inspiration, this time attempting to convince Chris Fabian to finally call it quits. The words he uses aren't necessarily so subtle, but you get the idea on this passage, which is steeped in resignation:

And with this ring I wed thee true,
And with this ring I wed thee now,
And with this ring I play so dead.

'Ruby' is the first of two seven-plus minute songs on the *Twilight to Starlight* disc, but it was actually the second to be written and recorded. At the time,

Corgan believed it would be the last attempt at writing a 'long and overly constructed, epic song', as he called them, but we know that wouldn't prove to be the case.

Opening with a lush piano piece, the early moments are then controlled by lively but unaggressive guitars, with some spacey synth added for further texture. 'Ruby' is also perhaps the closest the Pumpkins came to revisiting their *Siamese Dream* days, with some psychedelic elements filtering through on the wavy introspective verses. The guitar-heavy chorus could easily have competed with 'Rhinoceros' or 'Cherub Rock', such is its melodicism and addictive personality. The final recording contains no fewer than 70 guitar tracks, partly due to Corgan's ire at the rest of the band for failing to work on the song themselves. In the reissue's liner notes, he spoke of how if you want something done, you have to do it yourself:

> Because my attention was elsewhere on other tunes, preparation of the guitar overdubs was handed off to my bandmates, who spent a week coming up with very little between them. With our time running out, I added something in the neighbourhood of 54 guitar parts in 4 hours, if for nothing else than to show my frustration with them in spite. Not necessarily inspired ways of communication, but effective nonetheless.

At 7:38, 'Ruby' flies by in no time, the multiple and often experimental sections perfectly conjoining to once again make the song worthy of being called an epic. For an interesting outro, a snippet of the album's title track is performed with an acoustic guitar for the chords and a clean electric guitar for the melody. This would have made for a decent closer, but there is still plenty more to come.

'Stumbleine' (Corgan)

This relaxed acoustic number allows another interlude in proceedings, built up of single-sentence stories for lyrics in which Corgan deftly revisits many of the themes covered on *Mellon Collie* thus far.

With just his Ovation guitar, Corgan recorded 'Stumbleine' in his Sadlands home studio, originally just for demo purposes, but later decided to use it instead of recording a polished sequel. His vocals remain soft and light as his imaginary characters deal with loneliness, family issues and depression. There have been a few theories as to the meaning of the song's title, the only confirmation coming from its writer being that, in this instance, 'Stumbleine' is a women's name. This mid-disc saunter is nothing special, but it was given a nice upgrade on later tours where an amended arrangement was played by the whole band.

'X.Y.U.' (Corgan)

Deliberately recorded in several live takes, 'X.Y.U.' is the final truly heavy song on *Mellon Collie*.... A raw and gruelling listen for its entire seven-minute running time, the Pumpkins enter noise rock territory here as the brash guitars thrive off some repetitive metallic riffs, and the meaty drum and bass rhythm section provides chaotic blasts and fills. Corgan's intense screams welcome the madman back to the party, continuing his vendetta against his now former wife.

The title, when expanded, stands for 'Ex, Why You?', and it is tough to hear how a once loving relationship could turn sour so quickly. The following fraught lyrical passage reinforces Billy and Chris' plummeting association-

There is no going back, this wasn't meant to last,
This is hell on earth, we are meant to serve and she will never learn,
Bye bye, baby goodbye.

'X.Y.U.' came from a host of jam sessions, with certain sections evolving over the years. Even when recording the track, there were small parts which were changed on the spot, but it is musically where the intensity is really felt. In the latter third, a bludgeoning passage sees the tempo rise to a thrash metal-infused level of chaos, and Corgan emits some deathly growls, which hints that the Pumpkins' long-winded journey on this double album is finally catching up with them; a breakdown ensuing as 'X.Y.U.' is signals self-combustion. Alan Moulder called his experience recording the song as his single most exciting moment he ever had in a studio, and the images of the quartet laying down this monstrous piece would have been worth seeing first-hand. 'X.Y.U.' would not have worked with a cleaner production, in fact, it would go on to become better received when performed live instead of through this blistering studio recording.

'We Only Come Out at Night' (Corgan)

The next swerve comes in the form of a goth-tinged light singalong in which the Pumpkins go vampiric on us, choosing to only come out at night because 'The days are much too bright'. Utilising a harpsichord as the lead instrument, with tippy-tappy drumming and splodgy synth bumps providing the only backing, 'We Only Come Out at Night' continues Billy Corgan's deep dive into a mental collapse.

In February 2020, this random and fairly lacklustre song was used in an *Apple* TV commercial promoting their iPhone 11, of which one of its selling points was the camera's low-light capabilities. An understandable choice of song to use in a sense despite its lack of bite (pun intended), 'We Only Come Out at Night' reached new heights by charting at 20 on *Billboard*'s Digital Sales listings. Who said consumers aren't easily led?

'Beautiful' (Corgan)

The final stretch of *Mellon Collie* becomes more disjointed with each song, and in 'Beautiful', we hear the Pumpkins in a happy state as they celebrate pure love.

Corgan explained this piano pop piece as 'a clumsy nod towards the greatest band ever, the Beatles, who inspired such excess in the first place'; and while the Liverpudlians wrote some cheesy ballads in their time, none were quite so whacky as what Corgan came up with here.

When planning the song, Corgan wanted to include a psychedelic touch before Flood advised against it. Instead, 'Beautiful' trudges along with a whimsical piano riff that is impossible to be taken seriously. Perhaps that is the whole point. A duet of sorts has Corgan's vocals feeding through the left channel and D'arcy singing through the right, and when some guitar is brought in during the second half, the song at least becomes a little more harmonised. As bipolar and brilliant as *Mellon Collie* is, many let their feelings known of some absolute stinkers that made the album, and 'Beautiful' may just be one of them. A nice and happy The Smashing Pumpkins circa 1996 was not what people wanted to hear.

'Lily (My One and Only)' (Corgan)

A comical story of a love-ravaged stalker – yep, you read it right … No one could accuse Billy Corgan of not having a sense of humour, and he puts it on full show on a vaudevillian-style track where its narrator revels in his unhealthy obsession with a woman named Lily. In the end, he gets himself arrested and most likely handed a substantial restraining order, the story relayed over another amusing piano piece, and with an autoharp and a basic drum stomp not too dissimilar to that which is heard on 'We Only Come Out at Night'.

'Lily' isn't terrible; you just have to take it for what it is. Unfortunately, the continuation of sub-par songs continues to threaten a damp squib finale, or perhaps *Mellon Collie...* has enough credit in the bank for us to forgive Corgan for these latest entries.

'By Starlight' (Corgan)

A nocturnal ballad of sorts, 'By Starlight' opens with a wistful fade-in where double-tracked guitars forge some tasty tones smothered in feedback. Simplistic in its arrangement once again, 'By Starlight' begins with Corgan feeling hopeful of saving his marriage, but very quickly, he realises that all bridges have been burned and there is no coming back.

Despite the sadness surrounding its theme, there are some romantic melodies dished out here, the guitars swirling around the mix and building a rather absorbing atmosphere. The direction Corgan had envisioned for 'By Starlight' was based around a 1970s rock sound, referencing 'Luna' from *Siamese Dream* as his source of encouragement. Flood then provided his input, and Corgan praised the producer's ability for capturing the feeling of night-time in the album reissue liner notes:

Flood's great skill, beyond being incredibly sonically gifted, is that he seems to speak the language of the songwriter. He articulates back to the songwriter what the songwriter is trying to do. In many ways, he sees more potential in your songs than you do. A perfect example of that on *Mellon Collie* is the song 'By Starlight'. There's a version of us in rehearsal with these sorts of Nick Mason-like slow fills and strings that sounded like something off a Dan Fogelberg album. Flood fucking HATED it. He said, 'What's with all the seventies crap? This is a much darker song. Let me show you what you mean.' So then we ended up cutting this very stark track that worked much better.

'By Starlight' fades out almost exactly the same way as it arrived, bringing to an end one of the better songs of the final few. It has been an experience, to say the least, but after almost two hours, *Mellon Collie and the Infinite Sadness* is set to draw to its close ...

'Farewell and Goodnight' (Iha)
The Smashing Pumpkins indeed say 'Farewell and Goodnight' with this acoustic/piano curtain call where all four members assume the lead vocal role, on short sections to pay tribute to all who made this double album possible.

James Iha wrote the song; the lullaby feel of it is evidently more in his style than Billy Corgan's. The line 'Goodnight, my love, to every hour in every day/ Goodnight, always, to all that's pure that's in your heart' has Iha's stamp all over it, too.

Drawing both the song and album to a close is a charming piano piece similar to that of the opening title track, thus bringing the magnificent *Mellon Collie and the Infinite Sadness* full circle with a highly satisfying finale.

The Aeroplane Flies High (1996)

Personnel:
Billy Corgan: lead vocals, guitar, piano
James Iha: guitar, lead vocals, backing vocals
D'arcy Wretzky: bass, lead vocals, backing vocals
Jimmy Chamberlin: drums
Recorded at: Pumpkinland, Sadlands, Bugg Studios, Soundworks, Chicago
Recording Company- all Chicago, USA, Charing Cross Studios, Sydney, Australia
(Spring 1995-June 1996)
Produced by: Billy Corgan, Flood, Alan Moulder, Kerry Brown, James Iha, D'arcy
Wretzky
Record label: Virgin
Release date: 26 November 1996
Chart positions: US: 42
Running time: 138:53

> If you were to listen all the way through *Mellon Collie*, and listen through
> all the B-sides, and then read the booklet, look at the pictures, it does kind
> of accurately sum up our last two years. The mayhem, the madness, the
> sadness, and the happiness ... and the boredom.
> Billy Corgan

The Pumpkins rigorously toured *Mellon Collie* well into 1997, playing shows
all over Europe, Japan, Australia, New Zealand, Brazil; and an intense string
of dates across America.

With the popularity of the *Pisces Iscariot* compilation album and the overly
positive response to songs considered nothing more than B-sides, the band
decided their cult-like following deserved to hear a number of tracks that
didn't make it onto *Mellon Collie*. A small handful of B-sides were thrown
onto the five single releases, but there were still many more left in the vault,
so acting as a companion piece to its elder double album, *The Aeroplane
Flies High* boxset was announced. Containing five CDs headlined by the
original 'Bullet with Butterfly Wings', '1979', 'Zero', 'Tonight, Tonight' and
'Thirty-Three' single choices, each disc was expanded with a host of B-sides
and some interesting cover songs. Distributed in a vintage carry case similar
to those previously used to store 7" records back in the day, Virgin planned
to press just 200,000 copies of the boxset, but such was the overwhelming
demand more were made, although it continued to be labelled as a limited-
edition product.

The Aeroplane Flies High provides a fascinating insight into Corgan's
exhaustive wave of creativity during the *Mellon Collie* cycle, and as with
Pisces Iscariot, it was sure to throw up some hidden gems which many felt
should have been included on the album's final tracklisting. An anthology
delving deeper into the Pumpkins' more prosperous period, the boxset sold

around 300,000 copies and debuted at 42 on the *Billboard* 200. Because each copy was translated into single disc sales, the 1.5 million recorded purchases meant the boxset earned the Pumpkins another platinum certification.

Disc One: 'Bullet with Butterfly Wings'

'...Said Sadly' (Iha)

The only B-side on the original UK and US 'Bullet' single, James Iha penned another one of his love ballads containing slide guitar and fills influenced by artists such as Derek & the Dominoes and the Allman Brothers.

Iha's idea for '...Said Sadly' was a country duet, and he is joined by Veruca Salt's lead singer and guitarist, Nina Gordon. A fellow Chicago rock band, Veruca Salt, took their name from the spoilt child character in Roald Dahl's *Charlie and the Chocolate Factory* book, and the four-piece made their breakthrough in 1994 with their single, 'Seether'.

Iha and Gordon bounce off one another with lyrics structured in a conversational style, where Iha professes his love and Gordon hits back with fears of being unworthy of such affection. Predictably Iha in every way, this generally acoustic ride is sweet and safe, but it does fit best as a B-side and nothing more.

'You're All I've Got Tonight' (Ric Ocasek)

This is the first of a handful of cover songs the Pumpkins would undertake on this opening disc. Originally written by the Cars and featuring on the band's self-titled debut album from 1978, the Pumpkins keep only the lead riff of 'You're All I've Got Tonight' to devise a hard rocking take of a new wave track, which overdosed on synth and keyboards.

This is a thoroughly enjoyable rendition without doubt, full of churning guitars and heavy double-tracked drumming. Corgan's powerful sneer makes him sound like he is having a lot of fun recording, putting a contemporary spin on a song which at the time was almost twenty years old. The Pumpkins' version can be heard in the 1997 Val Kilmer thriller *The Saint*. However, it wasn't included on its later official soundtrack.

'Clones (We're All)' (David Carron)

Giving another new wave song the hard rock treatment, the Pumpkins next enlist Alice Cooper's 1980 single, 'Clones (We're All)'. From the *Flush the Fashion* album and his first Top 40 song in over two years, this era of Alice Cooper was long before he would transform his career at the end of the decade with the hair metal mega-hit 'Poison'.

With a theme of forced conformity, 'Clones' was rehearsed and recorded by the Chicago Four in a little over an hour, making the song their own with driving guitars, palm-muted riffs and boastful Chamberlin drumming. Some people probably haven't heard Alice Cooper's version, and you don't need to because the Pumpkins' better and vibrant take is all you need to familiarise yourself with.

'A Night Like This' (Robert Smith)
It was only a matter of time before a Cure song would turn up, a band hugely inspirational to Billy Corgan, but this is a very brave move, choosing one of the goth rock icon's best songs of the 1980s.

From the Brits' 1985 album, *The Head on the Door*, 'A Night Like This' sits neatly between gothic rock and new wave, and the Pumpkins give it an interesting makeover by slowing things down, adding some acoustic guitars, and writing different drum parts for each section. Corgan passes over the vocal duties to Iha, whose deeper refrains not so regularly heard find him a little out of his comfort zone. There is no love ballad here. Some cello work brings those expected gothic sensibilities, and the way the quartet refuse to play it safe by re-arranging this originally excellent song is commendable; and for the most part, their intentions proved triumphant.

'Destination Unknown' (Dale Bozzio, Terry Bozzio, Warren Cuccurullo)
Next, the Pumpkins cover the Missing Persons' 1982 single, 'Destination Unknown', first released on their self-titled EP two years earlier, before they caught the eye of Capitol Records.

The female-fronted new wavers were a minor sensation, but the lyrics to this song struck a nerve with Corgan, their content full of a similar doom and gloom which he liked to express – 'I have nowhere to go, I don't know what to do, and I don't even know the time of day, I guess it won't matter anyway'.

There are an awful lot of synths here, as well as other electronics and the occasional industrial blast thrown in for good measure; a 'techno vibe' as Corgan liked to call it, which had 'evolved out of boredom with some of the rock and roll-y things that we'd been working on'. Keeping faithful to the sound of the '80s from which 'Destination Unknown' was born, this cover is stimulating but not spectacular.

'Dreaming' (Debbie Harry, Chris Stein)
The final track on this first disc is one last cover; 'Dreaming' was the first entry on Blondie's 1979 album, *Eat to the Beat*, and one of many renowned power pop songs that everyone's favourite pin-up, Debbie Harry, penned during the band's career. This one was also partly inspired by ABBA's 'Dancing Queen', if you can imagine.

D'arcy sings most of the leads here, on a cover that is not quite so happy and breezy as the original. Smeared with trippy electronics and with drum loops where scratch guitars were recorded over them, the warped sounds make for a bamboozling listening experience, perhaps caused by reported technical problems which plagued its recording. This disc supplies a mixed

77

bag of cover songs, but as the box set continues, we are set to be treated to some original Pumpkins material worthy of the entrance fee paid to hear it.

Disc Two: '1979'
'Ugly' (Corgan)
Each disc's tracklisting appears to have been methodically put together. The 'Bullet' disc housed most of the cover songs, an easy decision as the official single only featured one B-side, and it is apparent from early on that the '1979' boxset disc caters for many of the songs that appear similar in style to the lead track.

The demo of 'Ugly' was vastly heavier and had the contrasting title of 'Beautiful One', despite having lyrics centred around one of Billy Corgan's favourite subjects – self-loathing. 'I rot in my skin, as a piece of me dies every day', he sings with a whole lot of emptiness, before continuing with 'I know nothing, because I am ugly'. 'Ugly' was, in fact, set to appear on *Mellon Collie...* until very late on, when the tracklisting was cut from 31 songs down to 28.

This is The Smashing Pumpkins in grunge mode. Corgan channels his inner Kurt Cobain while the moodiness of the palm-muted guitars and percussive beats amble, along with an atmospheric guitar rhythm providing a morbid undertone. Reminiscent of *Nevermind*-era Nirvana, there is an expectancy that 'Ugly' will explode into life at some point; however, it remains in a subdued state throughout its running time.

'The Boy' (Iha)
James Iha described his latest entry of personally penned songs as new wave, where he repeatedly sings the line 'I'm in love again' with a hazy vocal chaperoning his innocent writing approach.

'The Boy' features a drum pattern extremely similar to that of '1979', which is perhaps why the track was considered a B-side from the off. The breezy guitar and bass work, when combined with the drums, is like something from the Summer of Love, offering a nod towards Iha's main musical influences on this catchy little number.

'Cherry' (Corgan)
'I need a lover' sings Corgan – where have we heard that before?

'Cherry' is one of the strongest entries on *The Aeroplane Flies High* thus far, the zig-zagging guitar effect building on top of a clean and sombre lead to create hypnotic verses on par with Corgan's passionate and commanding vocal performance. The frontman admitted that one of his biggest regrets was not spending more time on 'Cherry', in fact, this recording is pretty much how it sounded at the demo stage, and it sounds perfect as it is.

It may have underwhelming status, but 'Cherry' possesses a charm and likeability, unlike almost any other song on the boxset. It doesn't speak of anything new, but it has an uncanny ability to draw you in and then refuses to let go. This is further enforced by a shimmering chorus, which draws a romanticism that is impossible not to take to heart. Wonderfully neurotic.

'Believe' (Iha)
An enjoyable lullaby again coming from the mind of Iha, 'Believe' is intended to be an uplifting song, but as its writer later discussed, it ended up having 'an undercurrent of longing, depression and sadness.'

A big part of that comes from the sullen strings that glide around the plush tones of an acoustic guitar, attributing nicely to Iha's delicate vocal. Following 'Cherry' was going to be a tough task regardless of what came next, and 'Believe' was unfortunate enough to draw the short straw. Luckily, its personality wins through.

'Set the Ray to Jerry' (Corgan)
Written way back when the Pumpkins were touring *Gish*, 'Set the Ray to Jerry' is a favourite within the band and one they wanted to include on *Mellon Collie...* but didn't because producer Flood felt it wasn't suitable.

As with 'Ugly', you are just waiting for the song to hit a higher gear, but instead, it settles into a customary flow where Iha's psychedelic two-note delayed guitar allows D'arcy to set the pace with a throbbing bassline. Jimmy Chamberlin supplies the adrenaline, his jazz background allowing him to beat and brush with an element of urgency as if he is trying to push the rest of the band into a rapturous crescendo that, for one reason or another, fails to materialise.

Corgan's lyrics revisit his 'I want you'/'I need you' love-drunk puppy moments, and while 'Jerry' is a decent song, you can immediately relate its tone to that of an early '90s Pumpkins.

Disc Three: 'Zero'
'God' (Corgan)
The third disc is presented in the original form of the 'Zero' EP, and has the heaviest set of songs across this whole box set. For those who hadn't heard its contents until obtaining a copy of *The Aeroplane Flies High*, 'God' is the song many had been waiting for thus far, re-igniting the fire with a punishing tirade of abrasive instrumentation.

Rivalling the fast and frantic cuts from *Mellon Collie*, 'God' was also intended to be an album cut, but it was felt that the drumbeat sounded a little too close to that of 'Bullet with Butterfly Wings'. The chorus isn't so anthemic, but it more than suits the nature of Billy Corgan's angst-ridden lyrics, summed up by the harsh passage of 'God knows I'm restless and weak, full of piss and vinegar/God knows we sow what we reap, in the dirt of grandeur'. Tracked during the album sessions and with the vocals and overdubs added later, 'God' is a groovy and welcome return to the best kind of The Smashing Pumpkins, and there is more of the quartet's signature rage to come.

'Mouths of Babes' (Corgan)

Bordering on heavy metal but closer to the style relayed over *Siamese Dream*, 'Mouths of Babes' appears to find Corgan dealing with the struggles of fame once more.

'So here we are, true superstars' doesn't need any second-guessing, his discomfort supported by aggressive, distortion-drenched guitars fuelled by stylish riffs. All four members snarl in their own way from beginning to end on this huge anthem, which sadly is a little too different from the rest of the material written during this time. 'The "dream" was a sham for saving what you can't,' adds Corgan, laying his frustrations on the table in the best way he can – by writing brilliant rock songs. It's a glorified highlight, without doubt.

'Tribute to Johnny' (Corgan, Iha)

A classy, blues-orientated instrumental- Billy and James pay tribute to Johnny Winter, who has long been considered one of the guitar greats and recorded blues rock albums up until his death in 2014.

This pulsating piece is steeped in distortion and fuzz, its crowning moment coming via an exceptional guitar solo that honours all guitar legends and not just Winter. Wiry bass and a pivoting drum section make this a full-band jam on a fun riff-fest, which further confirmed The Smashing Pumpkins possessed two of the decade's most stellar guitarists.

'Marquis in Spades' (Corgan)

Continuing the pace is the rampant 'Marquis in Spades', documented live on Corgan's eight-track cassette recorder and finding the Pumpkins at their rawest. It is in these instances you truly capture the band at their most cohesive and primaeval.

Corgan's vocals may be slightly suppressed by the searing instrumentation, but it's a minor footnote; however, the 'Angels, barbed wire, fuck you, desire' lyric is an agitated standout in keeping with the hostile nature of the music. Corgan liked the 'sheer brutality' of 'Marquis in Spades' and so did a lot of listeners, so quite what he felt was missing is anyone's guess as it only appears here in the form of a crushing B-side.

'Pennies' (Corgan)

A lighter rock track comparable to the indie style of the later '90s rock of The Cure ('Friday I'm in Love', for example), 'Pennies' was also recorded live and had some 12-string overdubs added afterwards.

Written in a matter of minutes, according to Corgan, this is a rather simplistic tune that supplies some calm after the relentless set of songs making up the rest of the EP. Titled 'I Stumbled Onto You' at the demo stage, Corgan appears to take aim at his soon-to-be former wife with this slightly humorous passage, which also risked offending his new lover:

It's a pity we're apart,
It's a shame you broke my heart,
But I've got a new girlfriend,
She looks a lot like you dear.

The band felt the first take of 'Pennies' was better than the one heard here, but the magic was lost forever as their engineer forgot to press the 'record' button when they began playing. The silly sausage.

'Pastichio Medley' (Corgan, Iha, Wretzky, Chamberlin)
In a bold move, Corgan decides to treat his fans to a small taster of some 70-plus tracks also recorded during the *Mellon Collie...* sessions- most of which have still yet to be released today. It's infuriating, isn't it?!

Between ten and fifteen seconds each, the riffs sound mighty and inspired – it's the ultimate tease. Virgin Records didn't like the idea of Corgan creating a double album, but perhaps they should be thankful they didn't have a six or seven-disc record on their hands, because these snippets offer plenty of promise. A dozen or so songs have gone on to surface on later reissues of both *Mellon Collie* and *The Aeroplane Flies High*, but the chances of hearing the rest appear to fade as each day passes. The finalised titles of all the tracks featured in this medley are as follows:

'The Demon', 'Thunderbolt', 'Dearth', 'Knuckles', 'Star Song', 'Firepower', 'New Waver', 'Space Jam', 'Zoom', 'So Very Sad About Us', 'Phang (1/2)', 'Phang (2/2)', 'Speed Racer', 'The Eternal E', 'Hairy Eyeball', 'The Groover', 'The Black Rider', 'Slurpee', 'Flipper', 'The Viper', 'Bitch', 'Fried', 'Harmonio', 'U.S.A.', 'The Tracer (1/2)', 'Envelope Woman', 'The Tracer (2/2)', 'Plastic Guy', 'Glasgow 3am', 'The Road Is Long', 'Funkified', 'Rigamorole', 'Depresso', 'The Streets Are Hot Tonite', 'Dawn at 16', 'Spazmatazz', 'Fucker', 'In the Arms of Sheep', 'Speed', '77', 'Me Rock You Snow', 'Feelium', 'Is Alex Milton', 'Rubberman', 'Spacer', 'Rock Me', 'Weeping Willowly', 'Rings', 'So So Pretty', 'Lucky Lad', 'Jackboot', 'Millieu', 'Disconnected', 'Let Your Lazer Love Light Shine Down', 'Phreak', 'Porkbelly', 'Robot Lover', 'Jimmy James', 'America', 'Slinkeepie', 'Dummy Tum Tummy', 'Fakir', 'Jake', 'Camaro', 'Moonkids', 'Make It Fungus', 'V-8', 'Die'

Disc Four: 'Tonight, Tonight'
'Meladori Magpie' (Corgan)
The 'Tonight, Tonight' disc contains a host of acoustic songs, a change in the tide from the breathless 'Zero' EP before it. 'Meladori Magpie' was first recorded during the *Siamese Dream* sessions and with a full-band involvement, but it is issued here with simple double-tracked acoustic guitar and an easy beat coming courtesy of a drum machine.

Corgan recorded the track in his Sadlands home studio when he was nestled into his lost love phase and using songwriting as solace. 'What had mattered, mattered little now, we had shattered apart somehow', he sings with dejection in his voice, and you can't help but feel sorry for the chap. The warping tones from the second guitar become a little irritating very quickly, and the song in general, falls a bit flat, suffering from the unenviable task of following the genius that is 'Tonight, Tonight'.

'Rotten Apples' (Corgan)
Another home demo that Corgan said he 'didn't have the heart or energy to go back and record', 'Rotten Apples' may just be the best of this batch of acoustic songs. Keyboard overdubs add an intensely gloomy backdrop, and while the line of 'Life just fades away, purity just begs, dust to dust, we're wired into sadness' is overly sombre, there is still a beauty to within 'Rotten Apples' that only a songwriter like Corgan was able to contribute. Emotion is the power here, and had the track found its way onto *Mellon Collie* it certainly wouldn't have sounded out of place.

'Jupiter's Lament' (Corgan)
Recorded on the same morning as 'Stumbleine', 'Jupiter's Lament' was later re-done with full-band vocals and labelled as the 'Barbershop Version'. This solo piece is what it is, just one man and his guitar left to his own thoughts, asking why his lover has left him even though he gave her everything he could. It is maudlin and underwhelming filler.

'Medellia of the Gray Skies' (Corgan)
The spontaneous 'Medellia' is considered a companion piece to 'Porcelina of the Vast Oceans', containing overly constructive and descriptive lyricism and dazzling guitar tones. Corgan's live vocal take doesn't come across so well, but the words he relays, only finished just ahead of recording, are memorable. 'And if I could, I'd throw away this world, I'd dress you all in pearls, I'd give you what you wanted,' he chimes over some densely atmospheric acoustic guitar which emanates sounds you didn't think were possible.

'Blank' (Corgan)
It's not often that Billy sounds uninspired, but he does on 'Blank', seemingly a little lost and recording just for the hell of it. 'I wish I was blank', he mutters over and over again, the lyric as weak and lazy as the slow-picked guitar that rides along with it. For such a perfectionist, it is puzzling as to why Corgan felt the need to put this one on show to the world.

'Tonite Reprise' (Corgan)
A rather unflattering fourth disc is saved by this stunning alternative take of 'Tonight, Tonight', recorded with a Gibson acoustic guitar. The lyrics may have been heard before, but they still cause goosebumps, and Corgan sounds arguably better here than he does on the fully arranged album track.

On early vinyl pressings of *Mellon Collie...*, the album was spread across three LPs and featured an entirely different running order. 'Tonite Reprise' was added to that pressing as track three on the sixth side and squeezed in between 'Lily (My One and Only)' and 'Farewell and Goodnight'. The track was removed from the CD and cassette release when the question was presumably asked, 'How much is too much?'.

Disc Five: 'Thirty-Three'
'The Last Song' (Corgan)
Entirely written after the completion of *Mellon Collie*, 'The Last Song' is not the last song on this boxset collection, but it could have been the last of that era of The Smashing Pumpkins.

A wholesome tune featuring a soft and clean guitar lead, flashy cymbal rides rather than an expansive drumbeat, and some subtle keys adding further depth. Its highlight comes in the form of a blues-tinged guitar solo from William Corgan, Sr. It wasn't intended for him to become a guest musician on a song, but when he was hanging out in the studio with his son the stars suddenly aligned, and the result captures a joyful moment which both men would be able to remember for the rest of their days. 'The Last Song' has only ever been played once live, during the band's 'final' show at the Metro in 2000.

'The Aeroplane Flies High (Turns Left, Looks Right)' (Corgan)
The best moment of the entire boxset arrives late into proceedings – an 8:31 blockbuster which is built around a moody grunge riff and the quartet's trusted quiet/loud shifts. It is when the volume increases that this track comes into its own, its powerful instrumentation combining from all corners over a strong chorus where Corgan snarls, 'I'm disconnected by your smile'. A snippet of 'Disconnected' can be found on 'Pastichio Medley', and here it is on full show on the revised title of 'The Aeroplane Flies High', laying waste just as the emphatic rhythm section does which rallies around it.

The track was recorded in two parts, the first during the band's tour of Australia in March 1996 when with some time to spare, they checked into Charing Cross Studios in Sydney. Jimmy Chamberlin laid down his drum parts there, and a few months later Corgan completed the song at Soundworks in Chicago, whereby this time Chamberlin had been removed from the band.

An extended and heavily distorted solo drives the final third, bolstered by further guitar experimentation and elevated drum swathes. It's a classic Pumpkins instrumental section based solely on sonic fury. 'I'll take my secrets to the grave, safely held beneath the waves, always knew I couldn't save you', sings a fiercely committed Corgan, which, with everything combined, makes 'The Aeroplane Flies High' one of the band's greatest B-sides. For any other artist, a song such as this would have been a contender for their magnum opus, but for The Smashing Pumpkins, it is another to be incredulously discarded and forgotten about for a while. Sheer madness.

'Transformer' (Corgan)

Also recorded in Australia in March 1996, 'Transformer' is a fast but fairly standard (for the Pumpkins) hard rocker. Multiple rhythm guitars play the same three-note lead, while D'arcy brings the bass groove and Chamberlin supplies some feisty drum blasts.

Lyrically ambiguous but based around a female being 'a real-life transformer' as Corgan puts it, this is a paint-by-numbers kind of track and an infectious listen, but the band playing it barely has to break a sweat in getting the job done.

'The Bells' (Iha)

The final James Iha contribution and, again exposing the night and day distinctions between his and Billy Corgan's writing styles, 'The Bells' goes a touch biblical on us. 'The bells are ringing out, what a sound, and I'm in love, the joy of love, the coming of Jesus' – a lot of listeners weren't likely to have expected that on a Pumpkins song.

Eric Remschneider comes in to play the cello and Adam Schlesinger of Fountains of Wayne guests on the piano. This was long before the New York rockers hit it big in 2003 when they dominated both radio and TV with their cheeky punk rock anthem, 'Stacy's Mom'. D'arcy supplies some backing vocals to Iha's dulcet lead, but all in all, 'The Bells' doesn't chime enough to live long in the memory.

'My Blue Heaven' (Walter Donaldson, George A. Whiting)

The final track of the boxset is a cover of a song written all the way back in 1924 and made popular by Gene Austin four years later when 'My Blue Heaven' was number 1 in the US charts for thirteen weeks. It remains one of the biggest-selling singles of all time, having shifted over five million copies.

Beauty is in its simplicity here, and Billy decides to keep this cover close to its original portrayal. Predominantly featuring piano only but with small string cameos to honour the time period from whence the song came, the parallel between 'My Blue Heaven' and The Smashing Pumpkins perhaps comes from the song's theme, which portrays the ideal of the longed-for 'American Dream', something of which relies on independence and salvation away from the chaos of inner-city life. 'What makes the world go round, nothing but love,' sings Corgan, something which he has been mirroring in his own songs ever since he first picked up a guitar and a pen.

The Aeroplane Flies High boxset comes to a close and there is more than enough content to consider the release a success. There are a handful of killer cuts deserving of a far brighter spotlight, but there are also a number of tracks that fail to light the touchpaper. *Pisces Iscariot* worked so well because the material was whittled down to a select number of songs and thus made for essential listening, but in this day and age of listening to music through streaming apps, there is certainly enough strong content here to be able to formalise our own 'Best of the Boxset' playlists.

The Transition

After the release of *The Aeroplane Flies High*, the Pumpkins saw out 1996 with an intense string of US dates. Sandwiched in between their 12th and 15th November shows in Chapel Hill, North Carolina and Tampa Bay, Florida, respectively, the band took a quick flight over to England to perform 'Bullet with Butterfly Wings' at the *MTV* Europe Video Music Awards. While they were at London's Alexandra Palace, the Pumpkins collected the Best Hard Rock Act award, fending off stiff competition from Bon Jovi, Die Toten Hosen, Metallica and Oasis.

In the first half of 1997, Billy Corgan maintained his comprehensive creative output by writing new material for both a prospective next studio album, and for a couple of movie soundtracks. These would further allow him to embrace The Smashing Pumpkins' transition into an electronic-orientated group.

By this time, it felt to many that rock was beginning to lose its mainstream appeal, and the charts were becoming overfilled with electronic artists. Even rock bands and musicians in other genres began flirting with electronic elements in their own material, and Corgan decided to follow suit. Having experimented on the unexpectedly successful '1979', and on a small number of tracks on the *...Flies High* boxset, the frontman didn't hide his desire in wanting to delve deeper into a new direction for his band, and his next fully-fledged attempts didn't take long to arrive.

'Eye' (Corgan)

Contributing an original song to David Lynch's psychological thriller, *Lost Highway*, found Billy venturing deep into electronic waters and moving farther away from the guitar-led heavy rock which had served The Smashing Pumpkins so well since the turn of the decade.

The movie's soundtrack featured choice cuts from David Bowie, Lou Reed, Marilyn Manson, Rammstein, and Nine Inch Nails – with Trent Reznor recruited to produce the whole thing. Lynch had also wanted The Pixies' 'Ana' as part of the project, but when he failed to secure the rights to use the song, he turned to Corgan at the last minute and asked him to bring something to the table. Corgan first offered a new track titled 'Tear', but Lynch quickly rebuffed it.

In the autumn of 1996, Corgan had begun collaborating with Shaquille O'Neal, the Orlando Magic-turned-Los Angeles Laker NBA superstar-turned-rapper, who was beginning work on his third album, *You Can't Stop the Reign*. Corgan worked on a Dr. Dre-inspired backing track for a potential song, but the collab soon fell through. When Corgan was asked to come up with a new entry for *Lost Highway*, he at least had a foundation from which to build.

For fans who were still digesting the intrusive and harsher tracks on *Mellon Collie*, 'Eye' is a stark departure from what people had been used to hearing from The Smashing Pumpkins. It is, in essence, a Billy Corgan solo song, recording the whole thing by himself, but as with most of these kinds of efforts up to that point, he continued to release them under the Pumpkins banner. Directly lining a 12-string acoustic guitar into a Waldorf VST synthesiser to create an overly shrill lead tone, and with a stuttering electro beat coming from a Kurzweil K2500 keyboard, 'Eye' is closer to Depeche Mode than it is the alternative rock acts of the '90s. With pulses throbbing and spitting underneath, this ethereal crossover may have been hard to grasp upon first listen, but the song soon earned enough positive feedback to inspire Corgan to continue down his newfound chosen path.

The first official song to arrive since Jimmy Chamberlin's departure, which partly explains the trial of a programmed beat, 'Eye' tells of overcoming an addictive relationship. 'Is it any wonder I can't sleep, all I have is all you gave to me,' sings a melodious Corgan, so as not to overpower the synth guitar. Lynch loved 'Eye', and he used the song during a nightclub scene in the movie – a weird and whacky picture starring Bill Pullman and Patricia Arquette, with a plot surrounding a musician who is convicted of murder.

'Eye' reached eight on the Alternative Airplay chart after the release of a single-track promo cassette, and six in the heavy metal haven that is, Iceland. Both the *Lost Highway* film and soundtrack have grown to be cult favourites in the years since their early 1997 releases, where, in the process, they summoned a new era of an electronic The Smashing Pumpkins.

'The End Is the Beginning Is the End' (Corgan)

There isn't much to say about the Joel Schumacher-directed *Batman & Robin* that hasn't already been said. The final instalment of Warner Bros' four-film series, and released in the summer of 1997, saw George Clooney replace Val Kilmer as the 'Caped Crusader', while Chris O'Donnell reprised his role as Robin and Arnold Schwarzenegger came in as the chief baddie, Mr. Freeze. The movie bombed, but its soundtrack at least managed to salvage a little bit of credibility.

R.E.M., Goo Goo Dolls, Underworld, and a host of hip-hop and R&B artists donated songs to the cause, but none of them were half as good as the sprawling lead single by The Smashing Pumpkins. Returning with all guitars blazing but also relying on vast electronic textures, 'The End Is the Beginning Is the End' is the first song to feature Matt Walker on drums; however, the enthusiastic blasts remain heavily programmed. Corgan and Iha supply strong riffs as the guitars churn and swarm – if this was the kind of electronic rock to come from the band moving forward, people were going to have no qualms whatsoever. Lyrically, Corgan gets into the mindset of the darker Batman character from the 1940s while also adding in his own feelings of the real world to create a fine balance between dystopian fantasy and global restlessness. One of the band's strongest choruses contains this memorable passage:

Is it bright where you are, now the people changed?
Does it make you happy, you're so strange?

And in your darkest hour, I hold secret's flame,
We can watch the world devoured in its pain.

The song was released along with a music video directed by Jonathan Dayton and Valerie Faris, with further input from Joel Schumacher. The Pumpkins can be seen dressed all in black, including Walker, who makes his one and only appearance in a video, and from this point on, the band would assume a rather gothic persona when in front of the cameras. The four play extremely futuristic-looking instruments over a backdrop of clips and images from the movie being promoted, and at the *MTV* VMA's later in '97, the video was nominated in the Best Direction, Best Special Effects, Best Editing, and Best Cinematography categories. No awards were won that night, but at the 1998 GRAMMYs, 'The End Is the Beginning Is the End' beat songs by Bush, Foo Fighters, Nine Inch Nails and Rage Against the Machine to win the Best Hard Rock Performance award. It meant the Pumpkins had won consecutive GRAMMYs in the same category after 'Bullet with Butterfly Wings' had triumphed the year before.

The extended single release contains several B-sides, the first of which is a slower and less rock-orientated rendition of the lead track with the alternative title of 'The Beginning Is the End Is the Beginning'. Also appearing on the *Batman & Robin* soundtrack, it was later used in a 2008 trailer for the *Watchmen* superhero flick, gathering some belated momentum which saw the song climb into the *iTunes* Top 100 chart. The song was then added to the Pumpkins' live sets for a period of time. 'The Ethers Tragic' came next, a simple instrumental solely composed of guitar parts, and then 'The Guns of Love Disastrous' revealed itself to be wholly made up of electronic segues.

'The End Is the Beginning Is the End' is, of course, the key song here, and it is a brilliant example of how electronic rock can sound when it is done right. It even made it to ten in the UK Singles chart; in fact, Europe embraced the song far more than America did. Because the tracks and music video were released through Warner Bros. Records, the Pumpkins were unable to use them for their own distribution at the time, but in 2005, all four cuts were included on the 114-strong tracklisting of the digital-only *Rarities and B-Sides* compilation. For what it is worth, Billy Corgan reportedly refused to give his authorisation for Virgin EMI to issue the release, which also contained *The Aeroplane Flies High* in its entirety, but the label owned the rights to all of the songs. The fans didn't mind because they were the big winners, and thus revelled in attempting to absorb over eight hours of jam-packed content.

'Christmastime' (Corgan)
Billy C. gets into the festive spirit on a track first demoed in his Sadlands studio in December 1996, before it was given a polished and classical production by Arif Mardin at The Hit Factory in NYC.

'Christmastime' was included on the third *A Very Special Christmas* compilation in late '97, released by A&M Records to benefit the Special Olympics, the world's biggest sports organisation for children and adults with physical and learning difficulties. Another solo song released under the Pumpkins' name, this piano piece speaks of a child's love of Christmas ('Christmastime has come, there'll be toys for everyone'), with some minor-key harmonics and sleigh bell backdrops to really get listeners into the mood for Santa. This heart-warming number joined tracks from Sting, No Doubt, Chris Cornell, Sheryl Crow and Enya on a gold-selling album which, like the two before it, were put together for a very special cause.

The Pumpkins embarked on a select number of European festival dates through the summer, including Roskilde in Denmark, Portugal's Imperial, and Rock Werchter in Belgium. The Chicagoans shared stages with Radiohead, Mötley Crüe, Skunk Anansie, the Prodigy and the Pet Shop Boys, to name just a few. On 5 December, the *Mellon Collie* tour cycle officially drew to a close at the Orange Bowl in Miami, in what would also be Matt Walker's final show with the band, on a bill headlined by the Rolling Stones. By this time, a new album was already well on the way to being recorded.

Adore (1998)

Personnel:
Billy Corgan: lead vocals, guitar, piano
James Iha: guitar, backing vocals
D'arcy Wretzky: bass
Matt Walker: drums
Joey Waronker: drums
Matt Cameron: drums
Recorded at: The Chicago Recording Company, Sunset Sound Recorders, The
Village Recorder (June 1997-March 1998)
Produced by: Billy Corgan, Brad Wood, Flood
Record label: Virgin
Release date: 2 June 1998
Chart positions: US: 2, UK:5, AUS: 1
Running time: 73:25

Adore was me trying to create a unique soundscape that was certainly
inspired by those moments, but at the same time, I had my own stamp or
take on it. It was a very particular kind of ruin. Using the Kurzweil keyboard
was one of the many tools that I used to make it almost sound like if you
found a record in the attic and said, "When was this made, 50 years ago?" It
was like trying to make a living relic of a record.
Billy Corgan

The remaining Pumpkins were still coming to terms with Jimmy Chamberlin's
departure when they began demoing new material for a fourth studio album.
Early on, Billy, James and D'arcy were in inspired form, feeling the chemistry
was still there and their bond reaffirmed in the wake of losing such a core
component of their successes thus far. Billy was surprised by the strength of
the initial recordings which took place in July 1996, but when he revisited the
tapes a short time later, he realised a lot of improvements were to be made.
The tracks didn't sound as good as he first thought, and so the session was
subsequently scrapped while Corgan returned to the drawing board.

It had been a painful time for Billy as of late. Not only had he lost his
best friend in the band, whose drum skills were impossible to replicate by
anyone else, but his marriage was now officially over. And then his mother,
Martha, lost her battle with cancer. From the outset, *Adore* was destined
to be a dark and deeply personal record, but what would its soundtrack
actually sound like?

Once returned from their European festival dates, the trio linked up with
Brad Wood, a producer whom Corgan had worked with when the Pumpkins
was in its infancy. The early idea for *Adore* was for it to be a live-in-the-studio
kind of album, and there was even talk of another double album when at
one point, there were 30 songs in the works. Cracks soon began to show,

however, when Iha and Wretzky's contributions were not to the standard Corgan had hoped, and when a similar disappointment arose from Wood's efforts, Corgan relocated the band to Los Angeles and took it upon himself to produce the record. Iha spent less and less time in Sunset Sound – the studio famous for being the home of the Doors and where they recorded their first two albums, as well as other esteemed artists such as Elton John, Led Zeppelin and Prince. Iha even refused to share the same accommodation as his bandmates, and Wretzky's interest was also quickly diminishing. Matt Walker was set to record all the drum parts, but then he became the subject of Corgan's ire. The frontman later spoke of his regret at how he treated his newest recruit:

> Matt had done a very admirable job filling in, and now, out of nowhere, I was turning on him for a situation he had no part of (we had even gone so far as to ask him to be part of the band, figuring at this point Jimmy really wasn't coming back). Everything that Matt did was suddenly 'wrong' in my eyes, and like someone who wants to break up with somebody but doesn't have the courage to just say "I'm done". I made the situation so miserable for him and me that it became a certain inevitability that he would go. Within just a few days, maybe a week of starting in LA, Matt was on a plane back to Chicago.

Adore, in this instance signifying 'A Door' to enter into a new era of The Smashing Pumpkins, finally began to come together when a drum machine was brought in, thus returning to how the band recorded pre-*Gish*, before Chamberlin came into the fold. The process was more organic, and for the time being, the three musicians were on the same page as the songs began to come to life. Heavily influenced by electronica and synth-pop but incorporating some gothic nuances to suit the mood of the material, *Adore* was going to be a tough listen for a devout fanbase who lived and breathed the feisty guitar-driven anthems of 'Cherub Rock', 'Bullet with Butterfly Wings' and 'Zero'. The mighty hybrid of 'The End Is the Beginning Is the End' had offered promise for the future upon its *Batman & Robin* release, and even Corgan stated how it would be the Pumpkins' sound moving forward, but the song would end up being a one-trick pony. Not everyone can easily embrace change and *Adore* was to be the ultimate test.

As the album grew closer to completion, Flood returned to help produce, mix and finalise the content. When looking back on Corgan's plea for assistance, Flood reminisced on his early perceptions:

> I came into it cold. I hadn't heard any of the songs; I just started going through them, and it was obvious that it was such an intensely personal record. It was going to be a solo record, but still had something about the Pumpkins in it.

Things appeared to be back on track until Corgan threw another spanner into the works. At the last minute, he omitted the album's closing track. In March 1998, Virgin were growing increasingly concerned at the direction *Adore* was heading in. Its content was too far apart from that of *Mellon Collie...*, and promoting it was going to be a struggle. Famed producer, Rick Rubin, was called in to assist in the studio and while Corgan refused to give up control of his art, he did agree to record one song with Rubin at the helm.

The upbeat and pure pop rock number 'Let Me Give the World to You' features excitable beats and fills from session drummer Joey Waronker, accentuating lush guitar melodies, which in general, were in stark contrast to the rest of what the album was set to offer up. The song has all the hallmarks of a '90s Pumpkins hit; in fact, its timing was impeccable and would have been a strong follow-up to the *Mellon Collie* singles. Virgin were set on releasing the song as the lead single, but Corgan feared it would strongly mispresent the album. The label refused to back down on their stance, and so the only way Corgan could suppress their intentions was to remove the song from the *Adore* altogether. 'It wasn't that I hated it,' said Corgan in a *Radio. com* interview in 2011, 'or even that I hated what Rick had done. He did a great job. It was more that I didn't want to blow up everything I'd done for this one song. So the song had to go.' It would be sixteen years before 'Let Me Give the World to You' was released in its original format on the expanded 2014 *Adore* reissue.

Prior to the disagreements surrounding 'Let Me Give the World to You', the relationship between artist and record label had become severely strained when Virgin sued The Smashing Pumpkins for alleged breach of contract, and non-delivery of albums. The band had signed a seven-record deal with Virgin on 12 March 1991, and come 1998, they had only delivered three studio albums. *Pisces Iscariot* and the *Aeroplane Flies High* box set didn't count towards the tally. Billy Corgan had seemingly put such wheels in motion when, in October '97, he told his bosses he would not be giving them any more records under the contract, effective of January 1998, and so Virgin filed their suit and sought compensatory damages, interest, and reimbursement of legal costs. They would still go on to release *Adore*, when upon the suit being made public, Virgin's attorney, Don Engel, quoted, 'Despite the existence of this suit, Virgin Records looks forward to releasing The Smashing Pumpkins' next album.' Less documented was the outcome of the grievances, which were presumably sorted out between the two parties behind closed doors.

Adore remained a bleak and introspective record. Nonetheless, it is an utterly captivating listen. *MTV* called it one of their most anticipated releases of 1998, and the reviews that flooded in were generally positive despite the stylistic changes. In 2005, Corgan called the making of the album 'One of the most painful experiences of my life', which is perhaps partly why he took its disappointing sales figures to heart. The album still went platinum within a couple of months of its June 2 release, having debuted at two on the

Billboard 200. First-week sales were recorded at being around the 174,000 mark, which wasn't too far off what *Mellon Collie* had done. *Mellon Collie* had greater depth, though, and it was the five singles which navigated the double LP to such incredible heights. *Adore* was out of the US charts in a flash, its early hype replaced by rapid despondency. It did top the ARIA album chart, though, and five in the UK was a strong result, all things considered, but the general consensus was that *Adore* was a flop.

Adore was still nominated for a Best Alternative Music Album GRAMMY in 1999 but lost out to the Beastie Boys' *Hello Nasty*. While *Siamese Dream* and *Mellon Collie...* became instant hits, the impact of *Adore* has been an enduring one. It is indeed a work of art, a collection of songs born out of loss and mourning, with emotions stemming out of each track which still feel as raw today as they did upon that first listen over two decades ago.

During an interview with *Esquire* in 2014, Corgan gave this vivid portrayal of life in The Smashing Pumpkins during the album's creation:

> If you look at the album *Adore* from the standpoint of a band, there is very little band participation on that album. It's beyond minimal. And D'arcy famously said to me at the time that it should have been a solo album. And that speaks to it. The band no longer had everything you need to have. And whether that had to do with Jimmy not being there or their hubris or mine or the combination of all the above – and God knows what else was going on, you'll have to read the book – whatever that was was no longer there. So, on some level, the album is really an artificial attempt to create the same type of sparkle and energy that the band used to give me. And now I'm in the lab almost completely by myself.

'To Sheila' (Corgan)

If there was anyone hoping the band's well-publicised change in direction was to be nothing more than a ruse, then 'To Sheila' may have come as a deflating realisation that The Smashing Pumpkins had indeed toned down. For others, though, the song served as a resplendent preface.

The electronic turn would announce itself in due course; instead, the scene is set by a tender acoustic ballad where the guitar and vocals were recorded live and in one solitary take. Billy wrote the lyrics to 'To Sheila' during a drive through Poland on the European leg of the *Mellon Collie...* world tour. There is no particular Sheila in question (nor would there be a particular Ava, Daphne, Dusty, Pete, nor Annie), but this veiled love song of sorts is a charming number revolving around the lead line of 'You make me real'.

With quietly picked chords and Matt Walker's minimalistic drum sequences, Corgan's captivating voice and poetic words are on full show, while Dennis and Jimmy Flemion from Milwaukee rockers The Frogs provide some neatly layered backing vocals. The Pumpkins have done acoustic ballads before, but 'To Sheila' feels different. Its importance in opening *Adore* cannot be understated. This isn't necessarily the calm before the storm, but it is a substantial shift towards something more elegant, inspiring and less contrived.

'Ava Adore' (Corgan)

Truly kicking into gear with the introduction of squelching synth and a chomping electronically programmed drumbeat, the moody and intriguing 'Ava Adore' exhibits the fully focused electronic sound the band had been building towards.

Minus any distorted guitar leads, there is a lot of love here. The lighter guitars and bass are meticulously looped and presented with an alternative kind of heaviness, while Corgan's snarl returns as he chastises the fairer sex. The line of 'You'll be a lover in my bed, and a gun to my head' lets his feelings be known perfectly, still bitter at his failed marriage, it seems.

The bulk of the song was recorded in one day, and while it was an obvious contender to many, Corgan was unaware of 'Ava Adore' being chosen as the album's lead single after Virgin were forced to change course upon the removal of 'Let Me Give the World to You'. He later spoke of wishing he had added something extra to the song, had he known of its intended heightened exposure. 'Ava Adore' is great as it is, though, and in its own way, it does rock hard. There is room for a small and semi-distorted guitar solo, and the sublime chorus is as strong as any other in the band's recent past; the troubling 'We must never be apart' lyric gaining strength with each sinister recital.

Released as a single on May 18, an inventive music video followed a couple of weeks later- a day before *Adore* hit the shelves, in fact. For the first time working with the British duo known as Dom and Nic (Dominic Hawley and Nic Goffey), who had been directing music videos since 1994 and had predominantly worked with Supergrass and the Chemical Brothers until now, the 'Ava Adore' clip was filmed in one extended take and is worth repeated watches.

The gothic ghouls of Corgan (Uncle Fester from the Addams Family, anyone?), Iha and Wretzky wander through a variety of extravagant scenes that are effectively designed to appear across one long hallway. Using both slow and fast motion techniques, Corgan's lip-syncing is bang on the money throughout; however, there was a danger at one point of calling the whole shoot off when certain issues led to long delays. Perseverance paid off, though, because the video is one of the band's best, and at the 1998 *VH1* Fashion Awards, the clip won the Most Stylish Video prize (for the flamboyant costume designs, most likely).

The hype surrounding the Pumpkins' return helped 'Ava Adore' secure decent chart success in America, reaching 42 on the Hot 100, three on Modern Rock Tracks, and eight on Mainstream Rock. In the UK, the song just missed out on the Top 10 by peaking at 11, while those dedicated rock fans in Iceland helped it reach number one on their national chart.

A combative and electronic-drenched anthem, 'Ava Adore' may not have been the heavy The Smashing Pumpkins of seasons past, but in the here and now (of 1998), it was vital in their new transition and is absolutely one of the band's finest songs, period.

'Perfect' (Corgan)

'Perfect' acts as a companion piece to '1979', immediately unveiling itself as a shiny synth-pop number very much similar to its counterpart. Charged by a consistently upbeat Joey Waronker drum sequence and light but catchy guitars, the song's title proves to be an ironic one as the lyrics linger around love and how it is anything but perfect.

Written during the Sunset Sound sessions, the song was a relatively late entry onto *Adore*, but its smooth and textured approach adds a little light to an album that proves to be overwhelmingly dark. It was even selected to be the second single, and ultimately the last, securing a 54 placing on the Hot 100 and 3 on Alternative Airplay. Reaching 24 in the UK maintained the Pumpkins' popularity across the pond.

In a bold move for its music video, Billy Corgan decided to try and bring back the original cast and crew from the '1979' clip, to further expand on the similarities between the two songs. Four out of the five main actors were tracked down (the other was in jail), and Jonathan Dayton and Valerie Faris returned for their fifth and final collaboration with the Pumpkins. The video follows the characters through their now adult lives. The most well-known of the four, Giuseppe Andrews, who starred in the KISS-inspired rock movie *Detroit Rock City*, as well as the bloody horrors *Cabin Fever* and *2001 Maniacs*, now has a wife and a child, and works a menial office job. When one of his friends steals from a James Iha-operated convenience store, a police chase ensues in which Andrews gets caught up, hitting the police car head-on. There is something hard-hitting about the scene in which Andrews' child is watching the aftermath of the accident on live TV, unbeknownst that his father is in the wreckage. For much of the video, Corgan sits atop a 150-foot crane, which he later revealed invoked a fear of heights. There is a small portion of live footage from the Pumpkins' performance at The Masque in LA, where if you look closely, you will see touring drummer Kenny Aronoff in one of the shots. In an ode to the '1979' video, another character leaves a cassette tape on the roof of his car whilst talking to a love interest on his phone, and when he drives off, the tape falls to the ground and gets destroyed, suffering the same fate as the tape containing the '1979' party scene footage from a couple of years prior. It was an interesting project to take on, but, in the end, Corgan didn't like how the video turned out, one of his biggest gripes being that he couldn't stop himself from shaking when aboard the crane. At the time, he was unaware he was actually scared of heights.

'Perfect' is a swooning alt rocker with glistening synth-pop overtones. Its impact was never going to be as greatly received compared to '1979', when at the time it found the Pumpkins treading completely different terrain, but as its younger sibling, 'Perfect' is a sentimental revisitation of past glories.

'Daphne Descends' (Corgan)
Nailing the electronic vision Corgan had been aspiring to, if there were a few more songs like 'Daphne Descends' on *Adore* then perhaps it could have reached multi-platinum status like its predecessors.

A haunting portrayal of the trepidation surrounding romance, the eerie ambience created by the effect-laden guitars and wailing samples work in perfect rhythm, as the heavier drumbeat directs the twists and turns the song takes at regular intervals. Corgan's wistful vocals give 'Daphne Descends' a gothic edge, while the lyrics, which are interestingly written from the point of view of a female, reveal how love can be inescapable at times. 'You love him, you love him more than this, and you cannot, you can't resist,' he sings with a sweet understanding, while nicely layered snarls roam underneath.

This is as rocking as the Pumpkins get on the album and it serves as a standout which is on par with 'Ava Adore' for the go-to track. For one reason or another, 'Daphne Descends' was never considered for an official single release; however, it was put out as a promo exclusively in France under the Delabel record label.

'Once Upon a Time' (Corgan)
The first of two songs directly written about Billy's mother, 'Once Upon a Time' is a country-tinged acoustic number that is relatively straightforward and further made up of soft brushed drumming and minute keyboard flutters.

'Mother I've tried, wasting my life, I haven't given up, I lie, to make you so proud in my eyes' sings a still grieving Corgan, on a song in which he described was penned... 'In direct opposition to my mother's untimely death. A message, I suppose for things I would have liked to have said but didn't have the courage for. A personal highlight, and one I treasure regardless of current taste or favour.'

'For Martha' would be the ultimate tribute. However, 'Once Upon a Time' has its own earnest charm, and while the song itself isn't one of the strongest, its beauty undoubtedly comes in its sentiment.

'Tear' (Corgan)
The song first offered up to David Lynch for the *Lost Highway* movie soundtrack, 'Tear' finally debuts here on *Adore* and it was most definitely worth the wait. After repeated attempts to record a heavier version, Corgan returned to the original rough mix because there appeared to be little difference between the takes, and in truth, 'Tear' is bold enough as it is in this instance.

Matt Walker's drumming sounds huge, but it is the orchestral-sounding electronics which give the song its dramatic and indulgent persona. Corgan's vocals morph with the increasing and decreasing music, his familiar snarl optimising the strongest moments, and his continually elevating lyric-writing quality delivers more exquisite passages. In many of the reviews for *Adore,* it was the lyrics that were particularly praised, and this emotionally charged section confirms why Corgan deserved such kind words:

I saw you there, you were on your way,
You held the rain,
And for the first time, heaven seemed insane,
'Cause heaven is to blame, for taking you away.

'Tear' is the last considerably 'heavier' song on the album, which is a shame as it comes relatively high up the tracklisting, and quite why David Lynch wasn't feeling this song is anyone's guess. It is much different to 'Eye', which, of course, did find its way into the movie and onto its soundtrack, but there is something about 'Tear' that has an edge over the standalone single. As part of *Adore*, it really elevates itself and stands out far from the crowd.

'Crestfallen' (Corgan)
The planned third single but later reduced to a promo-only, 'Crestfallen' is a generous piano ballad that finds Corgan re-evaluating his life in order to find its true purpose.

'Who am I to need you when I'm down, and where you are when I need you around' he protests on this smooth composition, containing minimalistic guitar effects which float in and out, and some low-key synths – just because. There is a slight trip-hop feel to 'Crestfallen', its tone and scenic drive coming across as wholesome despite its shy exposition.

Included in the setlist of the Pumpkins' summer tour of '98, the first performance of the song was significant for it being the first time Corgan had played the piano live and to a wider audience. 'Crestfallen' was also performed at the *VH1* Fashion Awards in late October, where the band also picked up the Most Stylish Video gong for 'Ava Adore'.

'Appels + Oranjes' (Corgan)
In a slight break to the measured pace of the album thus far, the catchy 'Appels + Oranjes' bursts out of the gate with an uplifting new wave beat and serene guitars fitting the change in disposition.

Not to be confused with the Pink Floyd song of the same but correctly spelt name, this Pumpkins opus provides an elevation from the doom and gloom whilst exploring reality. Billy asks question after question as he challenges the listener to re-consider their views of both themselves and the world around them, the 'What if's' piling up as each lyrical line comes and goes. The demo was actually titled 'What If', which is hardly surprising.

'Appels + Oranjes' was the first song written and recorded for *Adore*, but the early attempt was rehashed and involved Corgan upsetting his partners in crime once more when he chose to scrap James and D'arcy's guitar and bass parts so he could re-record them himself. Some things never change; however, Corgan did make the point of crediting his bandmates while trying to justify his decision in the album reissue's liner notes:

> While that might seem disrespectful, I fully acknowledge that I probably wouldn't have arrived at the final arrangement unless I had their original parts as a jump-off point.

There is nothing to dislike about this song; its atmospherics are harnessed by colourful synths and a commanding programmed drumbeat, which single-handedly energises the soundscape. It's a welcome mid-album curveball.

'Pug' (Corgan)
Described by Corgan as a 'minor key blues death march', 'Pug' lends some extremely menacing-sounding synth patterns to establish an apprehensive and noir-ish vibe from the off.

The song flows evenly without ever-expanding into more, its plodding tempo allowing less intimidating sections where the occasional guitar wail filters through to replace the tension for a short time at least. 'A tale of sexual misanthropy, no less dressed up as a delusional pop song' is the term its writer came up with to ideally capture 'Pug', but 'pop song' is a bit of a stretch for this peculiar effort. It isn't rock either; in fact, it is impossible to put a label on the track.

Later adding some futuristic laser pulses which overcompensate on Billy's electronic experiment, 'Pug' tries a little too hard to rival the Depeche Modes and Cures of the world. It's not one of the better moments on *Adore*.

'The Tale of Dusty and Pistol Pete' (Corgan)
Billy turns storyteller on this interesting folk-tinged acoustic number in which Pete murders Dusty, only for her to return as a ghost and haunt her lover and killer for eternity. The irony is just that.

Showing why Corgan was lauded for his lyricism on *Adore*, his poetic and striking descriptions do more than enough to keep the song on the right track. There is less reliance on electronics, as the drums sound more natural and in need of no digital enhancement, and the guitar chords thrive even if their simple arrangements help the song saunter along in a lower gear.

Moments such as this show there is still an alternative side to The Smashing Pumpkins, even if it is on the lower end of the spectrum, but 'The Tale of Dusty and Pistol Pete' is ideally placed in the tracklisting as we continue to be left guessing as to what kind of song will come next.

'Annie-Dog' (Corgan)

As a playful character, Annie-Dog is like many women I've met and found
fascinating, being among those who are willing to trade their bodies
so readily for something much more valuable; like say attention or the
appearances of love.
Billy Corgan

With droning piano and a standard drum march accompanying it, 'Annie-
Dog' has a grunge edge even though a guitar is nowhere to be heard. With
Corgan's quieter and intentionally flat vocals, the style of 'Annie-Dog' conveys
those from the early '90s, in equal measures bringing to mind Nirvana and
Alice in Chains.

Corgan is extremely adept at relaying his thoughts through complex lyrical
passages, and 'Annie-Dog' is another one of those moments where you
wonder how he comes up with often unfathomable sentences. The opening
monologue of 'Amphetamine Annie-Dog, has her leash and a face/Her velvet
spleen her shackle spine/Her diamond curse, it comes with mine' is faultless
in its gyrating description, even if you haven't a clue as to what it is he is
getting at. As grunge as the Pumpkins have been since *Siamese Dream*.

'Shame' (Corgan)

Considered by Corgan as one of the final recordings from the original The
Smashing Pumpkins, the pre-Jimmy Chamberlin line-up who used a drum
machine for its fourth member, it is perhaps fitting that 'Shame' is one of the
better songs on *Adore*.

Written in no time when Corgan woke up one morning feeling overly
sad, 'Shame' was recorded live and is a 6:40 therapy session which again
highlights power in simplicity. 'Hello goodbye, you made us cry', sings Corgan
recurrently, the tempo throughout remaining slow to let the dulcet guitars
glisten and gleam to their heart's content. The stunningly ambient textures
come with a small delay and make for a tranquil setting, and because of that,
'Shame' at no point feels overlong.

Doing what he does best, Corgan takes his sadness and puts it into song,
with emotional and musical support coming from James and D'arcy. When
the trio were on the same page, songs such as 'Shame' verified the magic was
still there.

'Behold! The Night Mare' (Corgan)

Adore continues to gather a second wind during its final throes, and the
excellent 'Shame' is followed by this enchanting number written about a
mythical horse 'that drives through your dreams', in Billy C's own words.

'Behold! The Night Mare' is fulfilled by swishing double-tracked drums,
piano, acoustic guitar and moreish echoed synth waves, when combined

together, forming a rich and spinetingling composition. The ambiguity of the lyrics plays second fiddle to everything that is transpiring musically, in fact, there is so much going on that repeated listens unearth something new each time.

The Flemion brothers and even Brad Wood are credited with providing additional vocals on this one, but it is Billy Corgan who deservedly steals the show with a towering display and easily one of his best on the whole of *Adore*. It can be said that it takes a softer and quieter focused album such as this to fully appreciate how good his voice could be. He has shown it in patches before, but on *Adore*, his progression and control has come on leaps and bounds from what it was on *Mellon Collie*. His range isn't to everyone's liking, but here it is perhaps helped by the phenomenal mixing, which makes the album a strong contender for the most complete-sounding Pumpkins record of them all.

'Behold! The Night Mare' is an imposing electro-drenched lullaby littered full of distinguished melodies, and it is utterly fascinating during its entire course.

'For Martha' (Corgan)

The ultimate tribute to his mother, Billy pours his heartache into an eight-minute ode where from its opening cyclical piano swirls, you know 'For Martha' is going to be a real tearjerker.

Matt Cameron from Soundgarden and Pearl Jam contributes the drums on his one and only appearance on the album, which, along with the piano, were recorded live and in one take. The combination guides much of the first half and is delicately crafted before some pocket-sized synth flutters move the song into its second phase. Out of nowhere comes a semi-distorted guitar solo, a kind of classic rock solo much like those heard on Queen's biggest hits, piercing in volume and positive in feel considering its setting.

'For Martha' then returns to the swirl of the tearful piano lead, before bowing out with 90 seconds of synth and guitar feedback, which doesn't really need to be there. Bon Harris from the electro group Nitzer Ebb is credited as supplying some additional vocals, having also programmed a number of the album's other tracks, but 'For Martha' is all about a son saying a final goodbye to his mother. Their relationship became stronger in later years and around the time of the album's release, Corgan spoke of being there until the end:

It's heavy when you have a son who's basically telling the world that his childhood sucked and his mother abandoned him. But she let me be wrong without saying, 'Fuck you, then!' We already had a great relationship and then when she became ill, she entrusted me to take care of everything. I became the parent and she became the child. That's the real beauty of life if you can enjoy it. It all comes around.

The lyrics are some of Corgan's least complicated. There is no need for tangent poetry here, just pure and unadulterated words from the heart. During those poignant piano refrains, this section speaks louder than music ever could:

If you have to go, don't say goodbye,
If you have to go, don't you cry,
If you have to go, I will get by,
Someday I'll follow you and see you on the other side.

Rest in peace, Martha.

'Blank Page' (Corgan)
Comprised of 48 individual piano chords, Corgan revisits his divorce for the one and only time on *Adore* via its unofficial album closer, 'Blank Page'.

Another ballad dictated by soaring piano, the first half is particularly sorrowful until some atmospheric synth inserts draw a testing period of the frontman's life to a close. 'I catch the rainfall through the leaking roof that you had left behind, you remind me of that leak in my soul' he sings softly and slightly scarred, although he doesn't sound as bitter as he once was. After fully coming to terms with the end of his marriage, Corgan wrote in his 2005 online journal how Chris Fabian was 'The best friend you could have for the last ten years' during the relationship. When she filed for divorce, however, he sarcastically remarked, 'She didn't even like my first album, the bitch.'

Brad Wood contributes some organ playing to 'Blank Page', so at least some of his short-lived work with the Pumpkins was salvageable before this reflective little ditty plays out with Corgan still singing over the dejected piano lead.

'17' (Corgan)
This futile seventeen-second piano melody is a strange way to bring *Adore* to a close, an extension of the guitar lead from a song titled 'Blissed and Gone' which was cut from the album because Corgan thought Rick Rubin didn't like it. It has never been confirmed whether Rubin's reaction of 'Whoa!' meant he did or did not enjoy what he heard, but it seems a hasty decision for Corgan to have scrapped 'Blissed and Gone' for such a silly reason. Quite why he felt this all too brief excerpt was worth including instead is even more bizarre.

Post-Adore

Instead of taking on a comprehensive world tour to promote *Adore*, the Pumpkins chose to scale down their travelling and take part in a fourteen-date trek across Europe, after which there were quick stops in Australia and Japan.

The tour was to feature the band's most extensive line-up thus far. Billy, James and D'arcy were joined by Kenny Oronoff, who had been the live drummer since Matt Walker had moved on. Hailing from Massachusetts and specialising in jazz fusion drumming, Oronoff's career has seen him play in the backing bands of Creedence Clearwater Revival founder John Fogerty, as well as the likes of Bob Seger, Lynyrd Skynyrd and Bon Jovi.

To further expand the live sound of the *Adore*-dominated setlists, percussionists Dan Morris and Stephen Hodges were enlisted, as was pianist Mike Garson, known for being part of David Bowie's band, The Spiders From Mars. The squad put together was indeed a talented one, but their personalities soon began to clash. Oronoff struggled to gel with Morris and Hodges, his drumming suffering from the percussionists playing on top and behind, which resulted in there being frequent timing issues. Mike Garson proved troublesome in his own way, refusing to play the same piano parts twice and often choosing to go off-script, much to the annoyance of Corgan.

After an appearance on the *BBC* music show *Later... with Jools Holland* (filmed on 12 May and broadcast three days later), the first official *Adore* tour date took place in Hamburg, Germany. As with all the shows, most of the setlist was made up of songs from the newest album; however, the occasional re-worked *Mellon Collie* song was also thrown in. There was no place for many of the band's classics this time. The performance was part of the city's annual celebration of the Port of Hamburg, known locally as Hafengeburtstag, and perhaps partly because there was free admission to the show, an expected 5,000 attendance turned out to be nearer the 25,000 mark. Whether their concerts were free or not, The Smashing Pumpkins were still able to bring in the crowds.

The most fascinating part of the European run was some of the show's locations, the band electing for some unorthodox environments such as the Cannes Film Festival, the Botanical Gardens of Brussels, and even on the roof of a *Fnac* retail store in Paris. There were some traditional venues also visited, such as London's Shepherds Bush Empire and the Olympia Theatre in Dublin. In Australia, the Pumpkins played a secret show at the Sydney Overseas Passenger Terminal, and in Japan, they were welcomed to the world-famous Nippon Budokan in Tokyo. The very next day, another secret show found the band setting up their gear on a flatbed truck and playing to students in the campus parking lot of the Kogakuin University.

The American leg commenced on June 30, the first of seventeen dates where the band donated all ticket sale profits to charities in the area in which the shows took place. Almost $3 million was raised, and here are some of the selected shows and charities to which the donations (rounded up) were made:

July 1 & 2, Universal Amphitheatre, Los Angeles, $432,000 to Five Acres Boys & Girls Society of Los Angeles County

July 7, New World Music Theater, Tinley Park, $500,000 to Make-A-Wish Foundation for Terminally Ill Children

July 10, Will Rodgers Auditorium, Forth Worth, $116,500 to The Family Place (helping victims of family violence)

July 20, Massey Hall, Toronto, $126,000 to Street Outreach Services (for the homeless)

August 1 & 2, Radio City Music Hall, New York City, $419,000 to Hale House (for orphaned children)

August 5, Ryman Auditorium, Nashville, $130,000 to the W O Smith Nashville Community Music School

On many of the dates, the citys declared a 'The Smashing Pumpkins Day' celebration to show appreciation for the band's generosity, while Billy Corgan later revealed the Make-A-Wish donation was one of the band's greatest accomplishments. At the time, it was the single largest donation the organisation had ever received.

On July 30, the Pumpkins were welcomed onto the *Late Show with David Letterman* to promote their 'Perfect' single. They played six songs on a stage which had been erected on New York's 53rd Street before the show was shut down by the NYPD due to severe overcrowding. The band's final performance of 1998 found them supporting rock legends KISS at the Dodger Stadium in LA. Taking place on 31 October and billed as the 'Ultimate Halloween Party', the concert attracted a crowd of 56,000, and rather than dressing up in scary or menacing outfits, the Pumpkins dressed up as the Beatles.

Machina/The Machines of God (2000)

Personnel:
Billy Corgan: lead vocals, guitar, bass, keyboards, piano
James Iha: guitar
D'arcy Wretzky: bass
Jimmy Chamberlin: drums
Recorded at: Chicago Recording Company (November 1998-October 1999)
Produced by: Billy Corgan, Flood
Record label: Virgin
Release date: 29 February 2000
Chart positions: US: 3, UK: 7
Running time: 73:23

> The goal was to take the digital lessons learned from Adore and apply them to a rock environment. How does one create the sound of a band playing on another planet? Through tape degradation, synth-like mechanised guitars, soaring pads and effects, heavily processed vocals, and of course, big drums.
> **Billy Corgan**

The *Adore* tour cycle was over in less than six months, by which time another album was already in preparation. Always providing more drama than a soap opera, there were more twists and turns to come within the Pumpkins camp when in late '98, Billy Corgan called a band meeting. An invitation was also extended to Jimmy Chamberlin, who had successfully sought treatment for his heroin addiction, and the drummer was welcomed back into the band. The reacquainted foursome decided to record one more album, tour it, and then officially call it quits.

The new material was already being prepped, and when the Pumpkins hit the road for a small set of club shows dubbed The Arising! Tour in April '99, audiences were treated to some early versions of songs which were set to be included on the next record. Beginning in Detroit on the 10th, the setlists also included a handful of classics ('I Am One', 'Zero', 'Today'), and deeper cuts such as 'La Dolly Vita'.

For a couple of weeks at least, it seemed from the outside that the band was back to its best, but things soon fell apart again. The last show of the tour at the Roxy in West Hollywood, on 24 April, would be the last show The Smashing Pumpkins would ever play with their original four-piece line-up. In September, a press release came out to confirm D'arcy had departed the band, who later said she had left to pursue an acting career. In 2004, Corgan revealed he had actually fired the bassist because of an ongoing drug problem. Not long after her removal, Wretzky was arrested in Chicago for being in possession of crack cocaine. Her relationship with Corgan had finally reached boiling point, and in the years since there had been some 'He said, She said' comments from both parties, but all that mattered now was that D'arcy was gone, and in the middle of recording what was arguably the Pumpkins' most important album yet. Some songs had to be scrapped in the aftermath while Corgan completed the rest of the bass parts. Wretzky did remain credited for her input in the album's liner notes. Hole bassist Melissa Auf der Maur, was officially unveiled as the latest Pumpkin, and she was present for all of the press and promo photos in the build-up to the record's release.

Although the end was nigh for the band, Corgan hoped *Machina/The Machines of God* would see The Smashing Pumpkins returning to the higher echelons of rock's elite. Their dramatic decline on the back of *Adore* clearly bugged the frontman; however, the musical landscape was vastly changing as the new millennium drew ever closer. A movement known as nu metal was taking over the mainstream by now, spearheaded by the groove-laden riffs and hip-hop-influenced beats of Korn, the potty-mouthed poster boys of rap metal, Limp Bizkit, and nine mask-wearing maniacs from Iowa known as Slipknot. Their music videos were all over TV, their songs were all over radio, and their albums sold in their millions around the globe. By the summer of 1999, Korn and Limp Bizkit had already topped the *Billboard* 200, and then all the major record labels scooped up any and every band who was on the rise, offering lucrative deals left, right, and centre. The gamble didn't always pay off, but when it did, the labels won big.

The Smashing Pumpkins had once been tipped to be the next Nirvana, but Nirvana's legacy only strengthened on the back of Kurt Cobain's death. While the Pumpkins were still fully alive, there appeared to be a distinct lack of interest in them by the end of the decade. The digital age was increasing and with music, movies and a whole lot else becoming readily available at the click of a computer mouse, people's attention spans were to be severely tested, and it made for cut-throat industries who would drop artists and bin records if the sales weren't there. Most bands would kill for a platinum album, which *Adore* was, but when it failed to become more than that, the Pumpkins' time in the spotlight burned out fast. Billy Corgan wasn't prepared to go down without a fight, though.

Machina found the band returning to their heavier roots. The guitars were reinvigorated and the drum sections at times ear-splitting thanks to Chamberlin's triumphant homecoming. Upon his return, he debuted a custom-made *Yamaha* green maple kit, and it was ready to take whatever punishment Jimmy would throw at it. The songs had clearly been written with every intention of being potential hits, though. They even sounded cleaner cut (Flood assisted in the album's production), and contemporary in order to compete with everything else coming out in the year 2K, whether it be the Korns and Limp Bizkits of the rock world or the boybands who continued to be pushed to the stars. For the first time, Corgan was coming off as desperate, and even his lyrics at times refused to hide a longing to revisit his band's mid-nineties heyday. One of the focal points of nu metal was the use of down-tuned guitars, and when the Pumpkins followed suit on certain songs, there was no getting away from what their leader was trying so hard to achieve.

His vision for *Machina* was typically bold, though, a concept album which early on he wanted to be another double-disc affair. Virgin had refused the same request for *Adore*, and after its disappointing sales, they were never going to oblige this time around. Less than five years ago, The Smashing Pumpkins were one of the hottest bands on the planet and making their record label a whole lot richer, but now Virgin had the control and they had evidently lost faith in the Chicago quartet.

The concept surrounding the album was never fully realised. Based on Corgan's alter ego, Zero, who renames himself Glass after hearing the voice of God, he then renames his Pumpkins bandmates The Machines of God, and their adoring fanbase The Glass Children. Just from those names, there was more than a hint of idol worship involved, with Corgan needing some reassurance that people still wanted him around. A 'pseudo rock opera' was what he had dreamed up, but the deeper themes of *Machina* were lost by the problems that marred its invention. There was even to be a cartoon to extend on the story, but that was scrapped before any of the already-filmed episodes could see the light of day. The project began to fall apart from the very beginning, and it's a wonder the album got finished at all.

Machina was eventually released on 29 February 2000 – a leap year. Reviews were generally favourable, the heaviness of much of the content receiving particular praise. Little to no feedback was given to the album's backstory. For some reason, *Machina* didn't debut on the *Billboard* 200 until March 18, but with sales around the 165,000 mark, it made it to number three. All things considered, that was a very good result, as was seven in the UK's album chart. Bone Thugs-N-Harmony's *BTNHResurrection* pipped the Pumpkins to second spot that week, but neither act could stop the relentless charge of Santana's eighteenth album, *Supernatural*, which had been released eight months prior but in total, spent twelve weeks at number 1 in the US. *Machina* quickly slid down the chart; however, it did scrape to gold certification. Even today, it is nowhere near reaching platinum status.

Corgan's fears of his band being no longer relevant appeared to be proving true, but the general consensus amongst fans is that *Machina* is a very good album containing some very strong songs. Had its tracklisting been void of a few fillers (the running time is over an hour and ten minutes long), the album could have been one of the band's finest works, but various details and subplots prevented it from being so. In a later interview, Corgan looked back on the album cycle and what he felt thwarted *Machina* from being more widely received:

I think the combination of the band breaking up during the record, D'arcy leaving the band... Korn was huge at the time, Limp Bizkit was huge at the time, so the album wasn't heavy enough. It was alternative enough, it was sort of caught between the cracks. And it was a concept record, which nobody understood. So the combination of those elements was a career-killer... *Adore* didn't alienate people, they were just sort of like, 'Oh, it's not the record I want.' *Machina* alienated people.

'The Everlasting Gaze' (Corgan)

Machina was marketed as a return to the Pumpkins' heavier sound and 'The Everlasting Gaze' is the perfect song to back up that declaration, as well as being the ideal choice of album opener.

An instantly abrasive guitar riff awakens the band from their *Adore* slumber, the shrill industrialised tone coming from the feedback relevant to the time period from which the song emanates. It wasn't the early or mid-nineties anymore, and Corgan knew he couldn't rely on the same trusted sounds to have fired his previous work towards multi-platinum status.

Whether serious or slapstick, his snarling opening line of 'You know I'm not dead' is evidence enough that he hasn't given up on his band just yet, and having his 'musical soulmate' back behind the drum kit provided assurance in continuing to push forward for the time they have left. Chamberlin makes up for lost time with a rampant performance full of offbeat hi-hat blasts, the demanding and unrelenting pace of the music further solidified by a huge and chugging bass line.

Beginning as a 'disco song' but thankfully evolving into a raging monster rocker, 'The Everlasting Gaze' begins Zero's transition into the Glass character. In a hasty but interesting passage where Corgan goes a cappella, he mentions 'The fickle fascination of an everlasting God', before again reaffirming he is not dead. At one point, the album's concept was to be biographical of each band member, but with D'arcy's exit, the one person who is continually revisited on *Machina* is Corgan, predictably. As with much of the concept, though, the true meaning of the lyrics get lost here, but it is the reinvigorated instrumentation that everybody tuned in to hear, and the song provides a breathless beginning.

'The Everlasting Gaze' was never projected to be the lead single; however, Virgin execs advised Corgan to release it in an attempt to rival the wave of nu metal which was taking over the charts. The track was ultimately distributed as a US-only radio promo in December 1999, serving as a fine introduction for what else could be expected from the album when it arrived a few weeks later.

A music video followed in the new year, hurriedly filmed in January 2000 while the Pumpkins were in London during a European tour. Directed by Jonas Åckerlund, who was part of the Swedish black metal band Bathory for a short time in the early '80s and would become an admired video director throughout the nineties on the back of working with Roxette, Moby, the Prodigy, Madonna and Metallica. Some of his videos would cause controversy due to their explicit content, but 'The Everlasting Gaze' was not one of them.

Filmed in an abandoned office, this is one of the rare Pumpkins videos to consist solely of a performance narrative. Melissa Auf der Maur is seen on screen for the first time as the quartet play in a large, bright, green-carpeted space before they smash up their equipment at the song and video's climax. It wasn't the most flashy or expensive clip they had ever put their name to.

'The Everlasting Gaze' reached four on *Billboard*'s Alternative Airplay and 14 on the Mainstream Rock chart, but gone were the days of securing Hot 100 placements. Corgan described the song as a 'Humanistic world view', while its razor-sharp instrumentation speaks for itself. Treading a fine line between hard rock and heavy metal, The Smashing Pumpkins had come out firing on all cylinders. Had there still been a wider interest in the band come the new millennium, 'The Everlasting Gaze' could have sparked a huge revival for the Chicago clan; instead, they remained bogged down in favour of a flurry of rap rock and post-grunge hopefuls. For hardcore fans of the Pumpkins, though, this was exactly the kind of song they had been hoping to hear.

'Raindrops + Sunshowers' (Corgan)
Jimmy Chamberlin remains in inspired form on this atmospheric Cure-like second track, which in some ways could be considered the lovechild of the '1979' and 'Perfect' double-header.

Built up of ambient guitar textures, scenic keys and Chamberlin's quickfire drum pulses, 'Raindrops + Sunshowers' fits the then-modern alt rock scene where even stalwarts such as R.E.M. were to dabble in electronic waters. This is a hefty departure from the opening 'Everlasting Gaze', but no one should have been surprised, because the Pumpkins have always been able to effortlessly switch gear with every passing song. Corgan appears to further react to his band's mainstream decline on the biting line of 'If you think they'll watch you now, you should know they won't, while the rest of the lyrics are made up of repetitive segments.

Lighter but still packing a forceful punch from the energetic drive of the drums, exuberant melodies from the clean-cut guitars create a direct link to the way in which the band transition from *Adore* and into *Machina*.

'Stand Inside Your Love' (Corgan)
Instantly aligning itself with some of the best singles the Pumpkins have ever put out, 'Stand Inside Your Love' is an outstanding rock ballad in which Billy Corgan writes about his then-girlfriend, Yelena Yemchuk. He even went as far as to say it is the only 'true love song' he has ever written, but it is the way he is able to incorporate the harder edge of the band which makes this a true gem.

According to Corgan, the lyrics were written within a matter of minutes and were based around the 'Who wouldn't be the one you love?' chorus line, and the passages that follow are some of his most openly transparent: 'You and me, meant to be, immutable, impossible/It's destiny, pure lunacy, incalculable, inseparable.'

Musically manufactured around Chamberlin's staccato beat and some infectious guitar rhythms where James Iha used an E-bow to good effect, the distinctive verses lead into an exultant chorus, which could not be more perfect for the radio airwaves. 'Stand Inside Your Love' was originally planned to have a similar vibe to '1979', but when the guitars fire up with the kind of distorted edge that is synonymous with The Smashing Pumpkins of old, this anthem is elevated to the next level. A screeching solo later takes centre stage, made effective by a Boss digital delay, and it is the final piece to this excellent rock puzzle.

'Stand Inside Your Love' replaced 'The Everlasting Gaze' as the official lead single, its appeal offering a stronger chance of gaining hit status. Released a week ahead of *Machina*, the song scored a decent 23 in the UK, while in America, it just missed out on the top spot of the Alternative Airplay chart. If ever there was a song to get the Pumpkins back onto the Hot 100, this was it, but there was to be no such fairy tale. Every track released in some kind of single capacity were considered failures.

Yemchuk played the lead role in the accompanying music video, directed by Englishman W.I.Z. and in tribute to Oscar Wilde's 1891 one-act tragedy play, *Salome*. The gothic sensibilities of the black and white mini-epic give the video its allure, which also features Armenian American actor Ken Davitian, best known for his role in Sacha Baron Cohen's 2006 black comedy, *Borat*. The video follows the patterns of Wilde's work, which depicted Salome's attempted seduction of John the Baptist through her dance of the seven veils. An extension of the New Testament story, which ultimately leads to John the Baptist's execution, the Pumpkins' take is similarly gritty but artistically evocative. The band themselves are seen performing in their own elaborate stage space, with Corgan wearing a long black dress of sorts like those he had been sporting since the *Adore* days. This did not go down well with the band's new manager, though, one Sharon Osbourne, who had only been working with the Pumpkins for four months at that point. Pulling up Corgan for his dress sense, which she called a 'try-hard move', Corgan refused to answer Osbourne's calls in the aftermath, leading to her quickly severing all ties. In an interview with *NME* in January 2000, having seen the video before its release, she talked of how Corgan's behaviour had left her feeling 'sick': 'If he thought I was a naughty girl, he'd give you the silent treatment. I don't need games in my life. I don't need stupid little boys making faces at me.'

At the *VH1* Fashion Awards later in 2000, 'Stand Inside Your Love' won the Most Visionary Video prize.

The song may not have earned the Pumpkins the mainstream success they had hoped, but it was embraced by their fanbase and hailed as a true return to form. It remains one of the quartet's most popular tracks, capturing the best moments of *Mellon Collie* and *Adore* to create a glorious rock anthem which, because of the time it was born, proved a little too polished for a new generation to accept. Corgan later revealed how 'Stand Inside Your Love' was the only song from the *Machina* sessions that wasn't changed from its original form – 'The band learned it, rehearsed it, recorded a rough version of it, and never changed a thing after that; which for us could not be more rare.'

'I of the Mourning' (Corgan)

'Radio, play my favourite song' sings Corgan from the off, in another clear bid of wanting chart success. 'I of the Mourning' grasps the darker side of The Cure, with ambient post-rock guitar tones generating a lighter but shimmering setting.

Throughout *Machina*, some of Corgan's finest melodies are on show and none the more so than on this song, where the music is completely captivating from the first note to the last. The noughties indie rocker would quickly become a favourite amongst fans, highlighted when the Pumpkins visited *MTV* Studios in New York on March 9 to perform on *Total Request Live*. Having already played 'The Everlasting Gaze', viewers then had the opportunity to vote via their phone or computer for another song from the new album, and 'I of the Mourning' was the overwhelming choice.

Underneath the overly positive-sounding music, there are moments of negativity that filter through in Corgan's lyrics: 'I'm home to die on my own' being just one moment where the writer clearly still has some demons to fight. But it is those grumblings of fearing to lose it all that Corgan talks of frequently on *Machina*, his Zero/Glass character an autobiographical one, and every so often, he throws in a passage just to see if people are still paying attention. 'I sit in the dark light, to wait for ghost night, to bring the past alive' captures a portrait of a musician and writer who doesn't want to accept the prospect of fading into obscurity.

The 'Radio' jingle becomes a tad repetitive after a while (it is the chorus after all), but there are some good changes during its 4:37 running time. After the second verse, a heavily distorted guitar solo ups the ante, and while Chamberlin's drumming is fairly substandard for the most part, he does unleash hell during a final section where he thrashes against Corgan and Iha's fiery guitar salvo. It is a joyous culmination which maintains the album's strong, and it has to be said surprising early rumblings. Also released as a US promo-only single in June 2000 but failed to chart.

'The Sacred and Profane' (Corgan)

As the first half of *Machina* continues to stun, it is apparent that while musically, the album is most definitely contemporary, it simply came out at the wrong time. There is no doubt in this writer's mind that had it arrived in 1998, either in place of or alongside *Adore*, *Machina* would have been a hit record. By 2000, though, the listening tastes of teenagers in particular had changed and if you weren't a rap rock band singing about doing it all for the nookie, or having fun breaking stuff, the more dense and creative music was beginning to get lost in the shuffle. This writer lived the nu metal movement, by the way, but he also understands its pitfalls and why it was so often maligned.

'The Sacred and Profane' is a magnificent next entry, at its best on an absorbing arena-sized chorus where Billy Corgan sings 'You're all a part of me now'. This isn't an arrogant statement; he never wanted to be a rock idol in the first place. Instead, Corgan appears to pen the lyrics as a message of thanks to the fans who have made the Pumpkins' journey so rewarding.

Another song that could so easily have been a single option, the memorable riffs and reflective melodies swoon on this mid-tempo love letter; in fact, the band would use the song's title as the name of their final tour ahead of disbanding. By the end, Corgan questions 'Will our love ever be enough', as if he is perhaps regretting his decision to call it quits. Either way, he is certainly giving us a brilliant parting gift thus far. Without doubt, it is one of the best tracks on the whole album.

'Try, Try, Try' (Corgan)

In a return to the synth-pop stylings of '1979', 'Try, Try, Try' offers some bittersweet optimism in overcoming adversity. Containing lighter guitars, this ethereal piano-led number allows a chance to catch your breath after the album's fully combative start.

Corgan is in a happier mood, encouraging his listeners to hold on during times of struggle. The line of 'Try to hold on and we are still alive, try to hold on and we have survived' surely has multiple meanings, one of them aimed at the band themselves.

It's interesting to think that much of the negative reaction surrounding *Adore* was down to it being guitar-lite, yet over the years, the likes of 'Disarm', '1979' and 'Thirty-Three' became some of the Pumpkins' most popular songs. The same can be said for 'Try, Try, Try', and in reviews of *Machina,* it was this track which earned special praise over the rest of the tracklisting. 'I of the Mourning' was planned to be the follow-up single to 'Stand Inside Your Love' but 'Try, Try, Try' ended up replacing it. Released on 11 September 2000, a year before the New York terror attacks changed the world forever, the song may have failed to chart, but its allure grew to be much more than just a hopeful radio hit. It showed Billy Corgan was still a highly accomplished songwriter and The Smashing Pumpkins to still be a set of dexterous musicians. They could have resorted to making a simple rock album before bowing out, but ten years after their initiation, they were still experimenting and diversifying their sound.

One of the main reasons the song failed to obtain any chart success was because of its music video. Jonas Åckerlund returned to direct the clip, which tells the story of two homeless drug addicts named Max and Linda. The content is graphic at times, as the couple thieve, and a pregnant Linda prostitutes so the couple can feed themselves and their habits. The visual aspect of 'Try, Try, Try' is certainly heavier than its audio counterpart. Linda later overdoses on heroin, and her unconscious state opens up a colourful dream sequence revealing the idea of a perfect family life. The video soon returns to reality and Linda is transported by ambulance to a local hospital, where Max meets her and embraces his love. The unborn baby appears to survive. Because of the video's content, it was banned by *MTV*, while an edited version didn't fare much better (it was only played late at night and received very limited rotation). An extended mini-film was also made, where an alternative ending has Linda passing away from the overdose. Such stories don't always have happy endings.

'Try, Try, Try' had a sole chart placing of a lowly 73 in the UK; however, its video did receive strong praise from those who were actually able to see it. The theme of the song is at least able to counteract the despair and uncomfortable viewing of the video, heightened by its dreamy piano and swishing synth patterns. A largely unheralded Pumpkins classic, with the band's '90s alt rock stamp written all over it.

'Heavy Metal Machine' (Corgan)
Along with 'The Everlasting Gaze', 'Heavy Metal Machine' is the heaviest song on *Machina*, but with a song title such as this, it was always going to be, wasn't it?

Boasting severely fuzzy and grinding guitars, meaty bass and a dynamic drum stomp throughout its mid-tempo presentation, there are certain comparisons to be made to the abrasive 'Love' from *Mellon Collie and the Infinite Sadness*. As with 'Love', Corgan's vocal is given a harsh effect, which makes his lyrics appear delivered with a hint of agitation at times, especially when he declares 'If I were dead, would my records sell?' Cheeky.

Released as a promo-only cassette, 'Heavy Metal Machine' does break from its toughness on another scintillating chorus, where Corgan offers to put his life on the line for music. This passage would make for a fine epitaph:

Let me die for rock and roll,
Let me die, to save your soul,
Let me die, let me die rock and roll.
Let the world forgive the past,
Let all the girls kiss the boys at last,
Let me go, let me go rock and roll.

It is a powerful statement, and the melodic hook is further entrenched in sadness because you know the end is coming. But when the next verse comes in with all guitars blasting away, this is classic The Smashing Pumpkins and they are refusing to go down without a fight. Flood was criticised for his production work by some small corners of the media, the overprocessed digitalisation of 'Heavy Metal Machine' being a particular sticking point for some, but when the Pumpkins sound as on fire as this, it is impossible to agree with such silly gripes. A killer cut.

'This Time' (Corgan)

A love song written by Billy to the rest of the band, 'This Time' is a beautifully reflective tune where the frontman looks back on their time spent together; a journey travelled with plenty of forks in the road, but somehow they were able to come out the other side relatively intact (minus D'arcy in this instance).

Written and recorded in a single day, 'This Time' is the only one from the *Machina* sessions to use guitar amps and cabs from both the *Siamese Dream* and *Mellon Collie...* eras; however, it is hurled into the 21st century with atmospheric overloads and elegant melodies befitting of the time it was devised. 'This time I need to know, I really must be told, if it's over', begins Corgan, in disbelief that he is putting his band to bed, the lyrics once again clear in their meaning. 'For every chemical, you trade a piece of your soul' is a specifically brave line considering Jimmy Chamberlin's past issues, also coincidental in the timing of D'arcy's exit from the band for similar reasons. Whether the line was written before or after she had departed is unclear.

Ambience bleeds from the guitars to create its sombre outline, but it is the lyrics that really draw tears from eyes. 'Someday we'll wave hello and wish we'd never waved goodbye to this romance, we'll drink up every line and shoot up every word till it's no more' is as powerful as things get here, a high point from a stunning pop rocker which sounds heavier because of its pristine mixing. 'This Time' quickly becomes one of Corgan's finest love songs, and he has written a lot of them over the years.

'The Imploding Voice' (Corgan)

Despite having a title that hints at a collapse, 'The Imploding Voice' has an overly positive message. 'All you have to do is play the part of who you are' sings Corgan, encouraging us to rise up regardless of what we have been through in our lives.

First performed live in April 1999 under the working title of 'Virex', that version was reworked into what you hear here, and like all the other songs on *Machina*, 'The Imploding Voice' was recorded in analogue. It's a hugely catchy number full of pop hooks. It may be a considerably paint-by-numbers track by the Pumpkins' lofty standards, but it is still more than deserving of its inclusion. The effect-riddled guitars sound mighty, often piercing in tone and volume, while Chamberlin's pounding beats help drive the ebb and flow.

Once again, finding the quartet striving for mainstream re-acceptance, 'The Imploding Voice' is one of those head-invading tracks that you will be singing to yourself long after it has finished.

'Glass and the Ghost Children' (Corgan)

If this was to be the Pumpkins' final album, then *Machina* deserves one of the band's long and winding epics. 'Glass and the Ghost Children' is that epic, the album's centrepiece, and at almost ten minutes long, it is made up of three powerful sections.

On an episode of Billy Corgan's *Thirty-Three* podcast in 2022, he discussed the track's story, which circles around a love interest of Glass, who crashes her car while under the influence of drugs. Treading similar lines of the 'Try, Try, Try' video concept, Glass later visits his love in hospital, where the lyrical passages then relay the drug-induced hallucinations she is having. While descriptive, the lines are extremely ambiguous, so if Billy hadn't revealed the plot, then it's likely no one would have understood what is going on; but as with many of his songs, it is the music which creates the true drama. Its opening section is experimental and rather proggy, the guitars, bass and drums emanating cacophonous sounds which, because the piece was recorded live, gives off the aura of a full-band jam. Corgan's vocals were added later, which is abundantly obvious due to the mixing. The second section is a strange one, where recordings of Corgan talking to his therapist about hearing the voice of God are played over a fine piano section performed by Mike Garson. It is interesting to hear what he is saying, and at one point, he even questions whether he has gone insane. And then, the final part begins, focusing on Glass' companion. Given a stunning soundtrack made up of hazy guitar melodies, spacey synth, and overall psychedelic rock sensibilities, which find the Pumpkins revisiting their *Gish* era, the sounds revealed make for an incredible finale to a highly creative piece of music. The three parts appear to hint at a death-rebirth-life process, whether that is the thought process or not, and while it isn't quite on the same level as 'Silverfuck' or 'Starla', 'Glass and the Ghost Children' is an excellent long-player which only someone with the mind of Billy Corgan could have come up with. At a time when rap metal was king, a track such as this was always going to be hard to digest for anyone other than diehard Pumpkins fans, which is a shame because the song and the album it is part of, deserve far more attention than they would ever receive.

'Wound' (Corgan)
The swooning 'Wound' is led by both acoustic and clean electric guitars and a pulsing beat. A handful of songs on *Machina* contain new wave nuances and 'Wound' is one of the clearest examples, the shimmering synth and keyboards forming the track's vibrant backbone.

Lyrically revealing how love is within reach of us all so long as we can overcome our failings and take responsibility for our own actions, this up-tempo rocker also contains one of Corgan's best vocal performances on the whole record. A standard album track but taking a different turn from the rest, 'Wound' is attractive enough to have been mentioned by some as one of their standout moments on *Machina*.

'The Crying Tree of Mercury' (Corgan)
Instantly bringing to mind the *Adore* song, 'Tear', things take a dark and dreary turn by way of 'The Crying Tree of Mercury'. Compared by some critics

to The Cure, the song overdoses on crunching synth and severely distorted guitar, which enjoyably grate on the eardrums after a while. The punctuating solo, while simply played, makes for a marauding back up to Corgan's continuous vocal flow in the final third, which only adds to the tension building towards its oppressive climax.

Corgan lays his cards on the table with lyrics once again seemingly aimed towards an adoring fanbase who stuck by him through thick and thin. With each passage, he finds a different way of showing his appreciation, but this short and to-the-point piece says it best of all:

> This love will stand as long as you,
> There's really no excuse,
> I did it all for you.

An internet-only interactive music video was released for the track by *MTV* in March 2000, as a way to promote *Machina* along with other ambitious routes Corgan took in order to spread the word regarding the album's concept. Directed by the frontman himself, the flash animation video had further input from Vasily Kafanov, who also designed all of the album's elaborate artwork. At the click of a mouse button, more of this imagery was made viewable after people had consumed this heavy electronic rock opus, where further themes of alchemy, astrology and spiritualism were just a few of which were explored in some form or another. Kafanov's art would also help *Machina* earn a GRAMMY nomination for the Best Recording Package in 2001.

'With Every Light' (Corgan)

Again, following up a heavy number with a dreamy pop/rock hybrid, 'With Every Light' feels distinctly flat in comparison to 'Wound', even if both songs come across in a similar style. Mike Garson contributes a sunny piano piece on this synth-dominated 'Spiritual epiphany' as Corgan called it. 'We basically are everybody that we meet, and the energy that sort of comes into our body becomes part of who we are,' he told *VH1 Storytellers* in 2000. However, with *Machina* reaching its final few songs and with an hour already on the clock, the theme becomes a bit too deep to justly appreciate or understand.

The guitars are minimal here, and even Jimmy Chamberlin sounds a little uninspired with his plodding drums. The inconsistent flow of the last handful of tracks doesn't help any of the songs' causes, and while it is nice to hear Corgan has a better outlook on life with the line 'Every light I've found is every light that's shining down on me, I'm never alone', 'With Every Light' is a strong contender for the weakest song on the whole album. Some of the negative reviews of *Machina* surrounded its long-winded running time, and while the handful of 'filler tracks' weren't especially named, this is one that could have made way without too many people missing it.

'Blue Skies Bring Tears' (Corgan)

There are a few songs in the Pumpkins canon that offer crafty hints of Billy Corgan's love of The Cure, but 'Blue Skies Bring Tears' is probably the most distinct confirmation of them all. The spine-tingling guitar parts could easily have been performed by Robert Smith himself, as the melancholic tones and effects sound extremely similar to the Brit rockers' *Disintegration* and *Wish* eras; namely the popular ballad, 'Apart'. Jimmy Chamberlin sets the pace with a disciplined drum stomp, while eerie synth patterns, screwy electronics and rasping distortion of the lead guitar combine as one to create a hauntingly gothic soundscape. Surprisingly, this version of the song is lighter than another take that is soon be unveiled, but 'Blue Skies Bring Tears' still possesses quite the onslaught because of its chastising use of digital enhancements.

Continuing the storyline of *Machina,* which is still hard to follow, the latest chapter revolves around a dream Glass has where he is a soldier on a battlefield as the end of the world quickly approaches. During an episode of *VH1 Storytellers*, Corgan extended on what the actual hell is going on with Glass:

He is so disconnected from everything that he seeks out love and connection wherever he can find it. The things he takes for granted, food, comfort and home, no longer exist. All anyone is asking him to do is kill and not be killed. In the dream, he envisions there is nothing left to put a name or number to. The way this ties into the story is that the world is coming to some sort of Armageddon and that he will end up like this character in the dream. The dream serves as not only prophecy, but destiny waiting to happen.

The song's title is frequently used in the lyrics, its morose sentiment fitting of the mournful but penetrable musical backdrop it partners. The soundtrack is dense and experimental, but as with 'The Crying Tree of Mercury', the value of 'Blue Skies Bring Tears' is somewhat lost because of how late it arrives, some 65 minutes into proceedings. The song is far more rewarding if you enjoy it as a single piece and ignore the surrounding interference, because musically, it is a brilliant and enthralling submission, and one of the Pumpkins' best songs post-millennia.

'Age of Innocence' (Corgan)

As if there wasn't enough content on tap already, Billy decides to throw one more song onto *Machina* in the form of 'Age of Innocence. A last-minute inclusion and another acoustic-orientated upbeat number, the song certainly does serve as an afterthought.

'If you want love, you must be love, but if you bleed love, you will die loved', sings Corgan, his positive headspace reinforced by gleaming synth waves and breezy guitar melodies. The latter half does gain in power, driven on by a potent drumbeat, which creates a minor selling point, but ultimately, the song is too innocent to leave a lasting impression. For a few months at least, people thought 'Age of Innocence' was to be the final Pumpkins song they would likely hear.

Still Becoming Apart

Released with advance copies of *Machina* at selected stores in the US, a five-track promo CD titled *Still Becoming Apart* contains an eclectic set of songs from various periods of the band's career. The first of them even pre-dates their formation.

'Hope' is a proggy guitar instrumental that first appeared on a cassette tape of Billy Corgan's earlier band, The Marked. Full of experimental chords and tones with a ton of reverb thrown on top, its inclusion under the Pumpkins name is a strange one, especially considering 'Hope' is the selection to open this twenty-minute compilation.

Dumped from *Adore* late on, fans were finally given the opportunity to hear the full version of 'Blissed and Gone' via this promo, and after just one listen it is obvious from the outside that the song should have made the album's final cut. This industrialised ballad features a pounding programmed beat, trippy synth, and a raw Corgan vocal. Some clean guitar melodies give the song a more fulfilling aura, while Cheap Trick's Rick Nielsen provides the additional tender rhythms during a brief guest spot, which only enhances the heightening sadness of the song's main lyric, 'Baby I need you around'. 'Blissed and Gone' is beautifully put together and is easily the main attraction on the CD, and its final passage appears to encompass everything Corgan was going through at the time of it being written, primarily mourning his mother's passing. Likely unintentional, the song becomes relatable to the time it was finally released – amid the band's final months together:

I had no voice, I had no drive,
I had no choice; I had no gram.
I had myself, I had my band,
I had my love, I had no hand,
In watching it all fall apart.
Maybe I need you around,
Baby I need you around.

'Apathy's Last Kiss' was a B-side on the 'Today' 7" single, a psychy acoustic-orientated number with a zig-zagging riff and flourishes of random guitar fuzz. Displaying lyrics surrounding the feelings of hopelessness, the song's high point comes courtesy of Corgan's brilliant line, 'What's the matter, what's the difference, you'll feel better if you lie, with stars in your eyes.'

A stunning acoustic rendition of 'Rhinoceros' comes next, and who else thinks of Prince's 'Purple Rain' when they hear those opening notes? The original *Siamese Dream* version is as close to perfection as you will get, but there is something just as special about this stripped-down take, from the spine-tingling guitar to Corgan's enamouring vocal.

The final track is a Soundworks demo of 'Eye', made up solely of a piano piece and a tender Corgan vocal, completely void of the electronics that souped up the version found on the *Lost Highway* film soundtrack. It's a decent alternative, which at least shows how the song came to be in the first place.

Machina II/The Friends & Enemies of Modern Music (2000)

Personnel:
Billy Corgan: lead vocals, guitar, bass, keyboard, piano
James Iha: guitar, bass, vocals
D'arcy Wretzky: bass
Jimmy Chamberlin: drums, percussion
Recorded at: Chicago Recording Company (1999-2000)
Produced by: Billy Corgan, Flood
Record label: Constantinople
Release date: 5 September 2000
Chart positions: N/A
Running time: 92:23

> I never thought we would see a near collapse of the music business and its
> dominated control on how music reaches people.
> **Billy Corgan**

Machina was intended to be another double album, and there was certainly
enough material recorded for it to be one, but Virgin flatly refused to release
it as such. The relationship between The Smashing Pumpkins and their record
label was fraught, to say the least, at this point, and the 1998 lawsuit had
left a bad taste in the mouth of Billy Corgan. When looking at releasing the
second instalment of *Machina* just a few months after the first, Virgin wanted
no part of it. By now, they were in favour of newly signed acts such as 30
Seconds to Mars, A Perfect Circle and Amen, so Corgan set up his own label,
Constantinople, to specifically distribute *Machina II/The Friends & Enemies
of Modern Music*. Being contractually tied to Virgin meant he was unable to
shop around for another record label.

The Pumpkins returned to the Chicago Recording Company in July 2000 to
finish the songs that make up the quartet's second farewell album, with Flood
assisting Corgan in the production and mixing. *Machina II* attempts to tie
up the loose ends left by its predecessor, while also being a surprise gift for
fans who, at the time, were still coming to terms with their favourite band's
upcoming split. No one knew it at the time, but the album would end up
being a far more rewarding effort than that which came seven months prior.

Classed as a double LP, *Machina II* was released alongside three EPs
consisting of B-sides and alternative takes. Continuing with the vague concept
of 'a rock star gone mad', the album was given an exceptionally limited
release- just twenty-five copies to be exact, which were sent out to friends of
the Pumpkins, fans within the online community, and one made its way to
Chicago's Q101 radio station. All who received a pressing were given strict
instructions to copy the music and upload it to the internet for the world to

download free of charge, in a bold move virtually unheard of at the time. By 2000, both film and music piracy was beginning to cripple their respective industries. With the continual evolution of the internet and certain software becoming easier and cheaper to install on household computers, even users with squealing dial-up connections were now able to download MP3 files in next to no time. Whether it be full albums or specific songs, for a music lover, it was as if a child had been handed unlimited candy store vouchers, and teenagers all around the world would spend countless evenings glued to their computer screens and sourcing copious amounts of music without having to spend a single penny.

Napster was the first big site to arise and dominate the free market until Metallica, Dr. Dre and the RIAA fought back and eventually shut them down; but it was too late by then and the damage had been done. No matter how many copyright violation lawsuits were filed, more and more peer-to-peer sites reared their heads seemingly overnight, spreading content in which a lot of it was yet to be released. The music industry was on its knees. Financial losses spread into the millions and billions, but it was the artists who suffered the most. Many were dropped from their recording contracts, and some even had finished albums shelved and left unreleased forever. Careers and dreams were ruined before they even began, and now Billy Corgan was supporting music piracy by authorising the global redistribution of *Machina II*. His intentions were different, though, on the one hand pointing a shiny and sharp middle finger to Virgin Records for not supporting his art, while giving with the other hand and showing loyalty to his fans for their undying support.

The sound quality of many of the album rips weren't great, but those who got hold of Q101's copy were able to hear it in its best form, the radio station naturally having better software at their disposal to make a cleaner rip. Given an official release date of September 5, reviews of *Machina II* were sparse and came from those who quickly downloaded the album before a flurry of other critics did the same. The feedback was overly positive, citing the work to be 'an artistic high' and 'a creative peak'. In a minor promotional move, the Pumpkins took part in what would be their final TV appearance on *The Tonight Show with Jay Leno* on November 17, playing a raucous rendition of 'Cash Car Star'. A fifth disc tying into the whole package was later given out to fans at the end of the final Metro show in December 2000, which contained live recordings from the Pumpkins' first-ever gig at the prestigious Chicago venue back in 1988.

'Glass' (Corgan)
Also commonly referred to as 'Glass' Theme', the opening song on the LP is a hyperactive two-minute rager that very few of us saw coming. Stripped of density in favour of an all-out attack of punk-fuelled riffs and raucous drum blasts, 'Glass' is bulked up by layers of rhythm guitars and bass to enforce its might.

'Shattering fast, I'm glass, I'm glass', fires a maniacal Corgan, his already vicious snarling lead doubled up with a distorted vocal effect. 'All alone in my soul, I betrayed rock and roll,' he continues over another harsh guitar drill, the song's urgency and carefree nature showing The Smashing Pumpkins at their commanding best. 'Glass' bows out almost as quick as it arrived, in less than two minutes, providing a lethal injection of heavy rock made all the more spectacular by the fact it didn't cost a damn thing to become in possession of.

'Cash Car Star' (Corgan)
Corgan goes on the attack against the music industry in 'Cash Car Star', whilst continuing the frantic, take no prisoners start to *Machina II*. Written during the *Adore* sessions but considered unsuitable for the general mood circling the record, Corgan decided to re-record 'Cash Car Star' and throw it into the mix here. Chamberlin's rampant drum performance was completed in one take, of which Corgan later revealed it was one of the best he'd ever heard from his musical soulmate.

The scornful passage of 'Everyone's gonna be a big star, everyone's gonna drive a fast car, everyone's gonna be in charge, 'cause everybody's business is everybody's business' highlights Corgan's naked contempt for an industry which by now was sucking the life out of his love for music, and as the lead riff crunches against the deep throb of the bass, even the synth backing which tries to relieve some pressure cannot overpower the riveting heaviness that is on show. The breathless performance of the song on the *Tonight Show with Jay Leno* can be seen on *YouTube*, depicting the Pumpkins as a fully cohesive unit in their final weeks of existence, and that same tight band can be found on the majority of this record.

The lead guitar and rhythm sections remain consistent throughout, but when James Iha launches a searing guitar solo, 'Cash Car Star' immediately enters itself into classic Pumpkins territory. It's another late gift that the world was very close to never receiving.

'Dross' (Corgan)
The proverbial 'hits' just keep on comin' as 'Dross' maintains a brilliantly relentless opening surge. A little more mid-tempo but no less heavy with its grungy riffing and pounding drum sections, 'Dross' again seems to find Corgan at odds with the modern-day music scene his band is involved in. 'You say I'm beautiful, well I can't help it, you say I'm empty, we all know I'm full of shit' he lambasts, touching on how quickly people can change their opinions on artists as they continue to follow the latest trends.

Iha's high notes strengthen this passionate thrill ride, and had *Machina II* been given a larger release, 'Dross' would likely have been a strong contender for an official single. It certainly offers more substance than 'Glass' and 'Cash Car Star'- even though both of those songs are sublime as they are, but this third track epitomises alternative rock when it is at its driving best. The critics who called the album 'a creative peak' weren't wrong, based on this incredible opening trilogy of songs.

'Real Love' (Corgan)

Across a handful of songs here, the theme of love is explored in a far more positive light than the battle-scarred Corgan has written of in the past, and 'Real Love' is the first of these. With a wistful vocal, thinly layered guitars, absorbing keys and sparking synth bursts, the track drew comparisons by some to My Bloody Valentine – another band that has proven influential to Corgan over the years.

The lyrics are structured nicely with generally ambiguous but poetic verses, while the hearty chorus lines of how 'Real love will listen', and 'Real love is painless' underline the song's overall intent. 'Real Love' was such a clear favourite of its writer that he included it on The Pumpkins' *Greatest Hits* album in 2001, as the only song from *Machina II*.

'Go' (Iha)

James Iha takes the lead on the resonant 'Go' and he never looks back. Largely consisting of squawking guitar tones instead of punchy riffs, 'Go' has Iha's imprint all over it both musically and lyrically. His tender and breezy vocals captivate as he details lost love, as he does in most of his Pumpkins efforts ('The slowest night, the slowest dance, you sway across the room as in a dream',) and it is a nice change to the album's flow but not too expansive to have it stand out from the rest of the crowd.

There are some gorgeous chorus guitar melodies amidst the occasional semi-distorted burst, further adding to this distinctive rock ballad, which in many ways acts as Iha's personal farewell to the band. As we get closer to the Pumpkins' disbandment in this book, everyone knows how Corgan would revive the group just a few years later, but Iha would not be part of the reunion. It would actually be eighteen long years before the guitarist officially re-entered the fold.

'Go' has only ever been performed once in the live environment, during the final Metro show in December 2000. Its poignancy may be somewhat lost because of the strength of the content in the album's first half, but 'Go' does highlight Iha's impressionable craft of writing some of the sweetest love songs in the Pumpkins' never-ending back catalogue.

'Let Me Give the World to You' (Corgan)

Some may have still been smarting at not having heard this *Adore* outtake, removed by Corgan when learning of Virgin's intention of releasing 'Let Me Give the World to You' as the album's lead single. The Rick Rubin-produced version would remain dormant for years to come; instead, Corgan decided to rework the track and implement some heavier and hazy guitars, a rich drum

123

pattern and some flourishes of synths. Its flow remains similar to that of the original, but you can instantly tell that Corgan's comments on it threatening to falsely advertise *Adore* as a whole were justifiably true.

'Let Me Give the World to You' is a romantic pop rock song, sweet and driving, and follows in the same vein as 'Real Love' and 'Go'. *The A.V. Club* called the song 'Prettier and more accessible than virtually anything the band has done'; whether they meant ever or just on *Machina II* (likely the latter) is unclear, but it is certainly one of the band's more innocent numbers of recent times. The original version would not see the light of day for another decade or more, officially anyway, but this incarnation of 'Let Me Give the World to You' was at least able to appease a large amount of an impatient fanbase who hated the idea of there being unreleased Pumpkins songs hidden away.

'Innosense' (Corgan)
Intentionally spelt incorrectly, the short and charming 'Innosense' is exactly that – a semi-acoustic singalong with some swish percussion and delicate piano. One of the least effective songs on the LP but contains a likeability from Corgan's calming vocal, sung in the form of a campfire lullaby.

'Home' (Corgan)
'Home, let the word spill from my mouth, love is everything I want,' declares Corgan on this album highlight. 'Home' very much brings Irish rockers U2 to mind with an arrangement forged by atmospheric guitars and ambient synths. The Pumpkins perfectly capture electronic rock in its finest form here, with all members of the band found to be in an extremely cohesive state (D'arcy Wretzky remains credited on *Machina II,* but Corgan could likely have played bass here); none more than Jimmy Chamberlin whose early prodding beats grow with each vivacious flourish. The final chorus, exaggerated by soaring instrumentation and sweeping melodies, makes for one of the most pulsating moments across all 93 minutes of the album.

Compared to the title track from U2's 1984 album, *The Unforgettable Fire*, with which there are some strong similarities, 'Home' is not an imitation, more a song concocted by an equally qualified set of musicians whose attention to detail comes over on a stirring and scenic electro-rock masterpiece.

'Blue Skies Bring Tears' (Version Electrique) (Corgan)
A much heavier version of the song found on the first *Machina* album and with not a Cure influence in sight, the 'Blue Skies Bring Tears' you hear here still maintains the apocalyptic themes of the original, but that is where the similarities end.

With a grinding bass throb, rabid guitars and explosive drumming all displayed with cutthroat precision, it is interesting to hear an 'alternate take' that is so far apart from its prototype. It's as if Billy Corgan decided to start from scratch, incorporating new lyrics that are equally as descriptive as they are poetic, with mentions of armies and soldiers and a final fight to the death. It's a further extension on the Glass dream established only months before; the line of 'Unleash the Armageddon, draw down the hungry prayer, kneeling for the final verdict, judges draw you near' sets to fulfil Corgan's comments on how the dream came to serve as 'destiny waiting to happen'. Dark and dystopian, 'Blue Skies Bring Tears' looks set to be the heaviest song on *Machina II*, until ...

'White Spyder' (Corgan)

'White Spyder' takes the ball and ramps up the volume through an abrasive combination of raw guitars and industrial synth crunches, creating an intense and ear-splitting listening experience. The riffs are metallic and bruising, as is Chamberlin's savage drumming; in fact, the term 'techno metal' has been used to describe 'White Spyder', and it more than suits.

Considered a sequel to 'Glass and the Ghost Children', with the song's prevalent lyric also referenced here ('and every little spider that crawled up inside her'), this is another mighty number reliant on fierce electronic vibrations and mass distortion. 'White Spyder' may be the heaviest song on this whole album while also being one of the heaviest songs the Pumpkins have ever written.

'In My Body' (Corgan)

Keeping up with each Pumpkins album having a longer-running 'epic', 'In My Body' is *Machina II's* flagbearer, clocking in at just under seven minutes and centred around a rhythm-based electronica sound to highlight its dreamy and trippy vibe.

The new wave guitars come with a small gothic sensibility that floats around the same repetitive riff, and the drums act in the same way, building tension to the point where you expect an elevation of some kind. Any potential shift soon subsides, though, the instrumentation settling back into its original flow with no winding subplots, which made the likes of 'Starla', or even 'Glass and the Ghost Children' so memorable. Billy Corgan's vocals sound like they were recorded live and then placed lower into the mix so the ambience of the music can be given full attention, but this could be dependent on the quality of the album rip you are listening to. Everything looks to be in place for another Pumpkins classic blockbuster; however, 'In My Body' remains in safe mode and loses its early appeal by hanging around for a little too long. It's a good song as it is, but it could have been so much better.

'If There Is a God' (Corgan)

The first of two versions found on this whole album package, the 'If There Is a God' on the LP, is a slow and distorted short player with an acoustic lead containing plenty of echo and reverb, its elegance emerging from an eerie undercurrent. The song's memorable moment comes from Corgan's very first lyric, perhaps a little tongue-in-cheek but fantastical and hinting at Bowie adulation: 'If there is a God, I know he likes to rock, he likes his loud guitars and his spiders from mars'.

A very short fadeout brings the track to a rather abrupt end after only 210 seconds, giving the feeling that Corgan may not have been completely happy with the song as a whole. It could certainly have had another minute or more to truly reveal itself and its intentions, but as it is 'If There Is a God' very much feels like an unfinished track thrown into the mix at the last minute.

'Le Deux Machina' (Corgan)

A less than two-minute electronic keyboard instrumental with an unnerving '70s or '80s horror film vibe, 'Le Deux Machina' – Latin for 'God from the machine' is an alien inclusion; its title perhaps offering the only relevance to why it was added to the album in the first place.

'Here's to the Atom Bomb' (Corgan)

Also known simply as 'Atom Bomb', and with further sub-headings of 'Alternative Take' and 'New Wave Version' on certain internet uploads, the final track on the *Machina II* LP can also be found as the B-side on the 'Try, Try, Try' single.

'Here's to the atom bomb, may everyone find a way to get on' sings a cheerful Corgan, amongst other hazy ramblings on a clean-cut alt rocker where the acoustic guitar trails behind the piano and an electronically programmed drumbeat. From the song's title, you could be forgiven for expecting 'Atom Bomb' to be another explosive number like the earlier 'Glass', 'Cash Car Star' or 'White Spyder', but instead, it remains relatively subdued.

For the most part, *Machina II* is a fantastic record containing songs you weren't sure whether the Pumpkins had in their locker anymore, but it does begin to falter during its final third. 'If There Is a God' is where the focus starts to become a little lost, and the handful of tracks that follow suffer from the lack of any real flow. The LP ultimately peters out with a set of songs that strongly come across as leftovers, but as the EPs would prove, there is still some strong material left to uncover.

EP One: (CR-01)

'Slow Dawn' (Corgan)

An absolute fan favourite, 'Slow Dawn' offers the same magic the Pumpkins had in the mid-nineties, with floating melodies, psychedelic guitar textures, and a hypnotic Billy Corgan vocal where he assumes the identity of Glass and observes the world from a distance: 'The midnight people washing down here, wasting away, they're gonna run the slow dawn awake.'

'Slow Dawn' was recorded on an ADAT, a magnetic tape format used to record eight digital audio tracks onto the same S-VHS tapes watched through VCRs back in the '90s (remember those?); before being transferred to analogue for the inclusion of vocals and overdubs. Recorded sometime between late 1998 and the summer of 1999, 'Slow Dawn' builds to an enthralling crescendo, prompted by a blistering guitar solo reminiscent of those found on *Siamese Dream*. The musicianship is powerful and the band sound super hungry, but as with many times before, a song as good as 'Slow Dawn' found itself being relegated to B-side status when it really should not have been. One of the best tracks to come from the whole *Machina* project.

'Vanity' (Corgan)

A free-flowing alt rocker written by Corgan as he considers the repercussions of vanity and its impact on people, and perhaps even a band – considering the state of the Pumpkins at this point.

Vanity stands at my door,
Vanity cries, why?
Vanity wants everything and more,
Vanity must die.'

'Vanity' is consistently paced and succeeds through the anthemic guitars and Jimmy Chamberlin's energetic and rhythmic drumming. There is also a nice little solo thrown in for good measure, but unlike the inspiring 'Slow Dawn' before it, 'Vanity' doesn't quite make the cut for the album and so correctly takes its place on this first EP instead.

'Saturnine' (Corgan)

Another *Adore* outtake, 'Saturnine' is one of those Pumpkins songs which gets better with each version recorded and released over the years. The first time people got to hear the song was on this EP, the song's title meaning 'Gloomy' and certainly taking a dark turn where the deep and distorted guitars mould with stiflingly evil-sounding synth jousts. Gloomy isn't the word, to be honest. In fact, the Armageddon Glass speaks of earlier in the concept seems to come in the form of 'Saturnine', with this version offering one of the band's darkest-ever songs.

A different recording was used on the *Judas Ø* rarities disc, which was released with certain editions of the *Rotten Apples* compilation album in 2001 and makes for far better listening, as do the alternative mixes on the later *Adore* reissue. Still led by powerful synths and electronically programmed drumming, each version of 'Saturnine' progresses to the point where it becomes another gem in the long list of Pumpkins classics, and while it is at its most commanding on the *Machina II* entry, go and check out the others to hear the song in its finest form.

'Glass' Theme' (Corgan)

Known as the 'Alternate Version' or 'Spacey Version', this rendition of 'Glass' has an extremely live feel and could even have been captured in the band's rehearsal space. It is certainly rawer than that, which opens up the LP; however, there is more focus on the emphatic drumming here, with the guitars lower in the mix. Still, the whole mood of the recording makes for imperative listening, and it is just as good as the original version.

EP Two: (CR-02)

'Soul Power' (James Brown)

In their long-running tradition of taking someone else's song and making it their own, the Pumpkins choose to cover James Brown's 'Soul Power, and they replace funk and soul with a stinging brand of contemporary rock.

First released in 1971 by Brown and his band, the J.B.'s, and acting as an ideal dancefloor-filler for years on end, the only environment you may move to the Chicago quartet's rousing cover is in a mosh pit, its jarring tone and ferocious Corgan vocal a million miles away from the original. Brown's fanbase surely disapproved of it, but the Pumpkins community firmly embraced it, and some may not have even been aware it was a cover in the first place.

'Cash Car Star' (Version 1/Alternate Take) (Corgan)

Fairly close to the version on the LP, the guitars sound a little cleaner here and the whole composition comes across as more radio-friendly, but in general, there isn't enough of a difference to warrant a second inclusion of 'Cash Car Star'.

'Lucky 13' (Corgan)

'Lucky 13' is a bruising and metallic romp where Corgan announces, 'I'm no good as the prodigal son'. Displaying the perfect union of Corgan's guitar playing and Chamberlin's expansive drumming, the 'musical soulmates' bounce off one another with a cacophony of down-tuned riffs and rolling beats.

This is another high point across the whole of the *Machina II* package, with a chorus as strong as any other from the quartet's past. Even in the year 2000, The Smashing Pumpkins were still providing strength in depth, and the late arrival of 'Lucky 13' justifies the decision to release these EPs alongside the full record.

'Speed Kills (But Beauty Lives Forever)' (Corgan)

Those who bought a copy of the 'Try, Try, Try' CD single would have been first introduced to the brilliant 'Speed Kills', in this instance the song being a haunting, five-minute Cure-esque composition. It remains the preferred version by the majority of the Pumpkins' fanbase; however, this second EP offers a heavier guitar-driven option, which is just as emotionally charged and contains a standout Corgan vocal performance.

'Speed Kills' seemingly paints a lyrical picture of Glass' relationship with the same love interest that was first touched upon in 'Glass and the Ghost Children'. The song's title is likely in reference to the drug she is addicted to, while the following excerpt is beautifully put together and perfectly entwines with the sad nature of the guitars:

First time that I ever saw you,
Crashing hard through days of pain,

You were one of God's children,
Left to cry out in the rain,
Waiting to be saved again.

'Speed Kills' is the final song covering the *Machina* concept, but being a B-side, it isn't clear where it fits into the overall story. On its own, though, it is a stunning song (both versions are), culminating with the last great Corgan lyric before the Pumpkins' disbandment:

When I ride with you tonight,
We can move at the speed of light,
Forever young, forever blind,
Into the stars we rock tonight.

EP Three: (CR-03)

'If There Is a God' (Corgan)

A second outing for 'If There Is a God', this version consists of Corgan and his piano. The original song isn't one of the greatest, so including this recording feels like nothing more than overkill.

'Try' (Version 1/Alternate Take) (Corgan)

An acoustic guitar and a repeated keyboard piece replace the piano-synths-electric guitar format of the renowned *Machina* single, naturally making this version of 'Try, Try, Try' stripped and sparse by comparison. It's worth a listen every so often.

'Heavy Metal Machine' (Version 1/Alternate Mix) (Corgan)

If it wasn't for Billy Corgan's instantly recognisable vocal style, you could easily mistake this alternate version of 'Heavy Metal Machine' for being a Nine Inch Nails song. Chamberlin's drumming is brash and heavily industrialised, the guitars are overly fuzzy and Corgan's vocal has a disjointed effect thrown on top, but you can tell this is an early recording and nowhere near complete. The excellent 'Let me die for rock and roll' chorus doesn't feature here, in its place, alternative lyrical passages, which were obviously replaced by the aforementioned later on.

If indeed this was the first incarnation of 'Heavy Metal Machine', then we can forgive Billy for putting it on this third EP, revealing its origins before being thoroughly overhauled into that which was presented on the first *Machina* record.

Further B-Sides/Cover Songs (In Chronological Order)

'Jackie Blue' (Steve Cash, Larry Lee)
The Pumpkins covered this Ozark Mountain Daredevils song in 1989, recorded at Solid Sound Studios in Chicago. 'Jackie Blue' was originally released by the Missouri southern rockers on their 1974 sophomore album, *It'll Shine When It Shines*, and as a single, it scored the band's second hit by reaching number 3 on the Hot 100. Utilising the same composition but substituting the country twang with feisty guitar fuzz, the Pumpkins' heavier take fully captures their kill-or-be-killed attitude in those early days.

In 1991, 'Jackie Blue' was featured on the Pravda Records compilation, *20 Explosive Dynamic Super Smash Hit Explosions!,* alongside lesser-known artists such as The Farmers, Spies Who Surf and The Sneetches, covering similarly obscure songs from the '70s.

'Terrapin' (Syd Barrett)
'Terrapin' was included on Syd Barrett's debut solo album, *The Madcap Laughs*, in 1970, his first release since leaving the band he co-founded – the future prog rock legends Pink Floyd.

This live recording is taken from the Pumpkins' visit to Chicago's Rose Records in June 1991, where James Iha sings the lead and Billy Corgan provides the backing vocals. D'arcy contributes some barely audible bass, while Jimmy Chamberlin taps away on some handpans. There are various clips online in which the band perform a heavier configuration, where in the full concert environment, it makes for better listening. 'Terrapin' was a B-side on the UK and Dutch 10 inch release of 'I Am One'.

'Bullet Train to Osaka' (Corgan)
Also, on the same 'I Am One' single, 'Bullet Train to Osaka' is an enjoyable instrumental which shows the band's talent for taking on a vast array of styles. With a little bit of surf, psych, blues and classic rock thrown together with a bit of Doors-esque organ, this catchy low-fi romp is extremely fun to listen to.

'French Movie Theme' (Corgan)
Written during the *Siamese Dream* sessions and chosen to back up 'Cherub Rock' on the 12" single, 'French Movie Theme' is a romantic-sounding piece made up of a pretty piano section and acoustic guitar, but despite its tone, the band saw this frequent rehearsal track as a joke, with the lyrics amounting to repeated 'Yeah, yeah, yeah yeah's' and the occasional 'Bonjour'. And that's about it.

'The Star-Spangled Banner' (John Stafford Smith, Francis Scott Key)
The Pumpkins cover their country's national anthem. Also a B-side on the CD and 12" 'Cherub Rock' single.

'Purr Snickety' (Corgan)

A sweet acoustic ballad from Corgan as he continued to find his feet as a young songwriter, 'Purr Snickety' contains the affectionate line of 'I'm your pillar of stone, so when the wind calls you to roam, you can call this house your home, only you'. Written during the *Gish* sessions but omitted from the album, this gentle serenade later acted as the sole B-side on the 7" release of 'Cherub Rock'.

'Glynis' (Corgan)

This is a lovely dedication to Glynis Johnson, the bassist of Chicago blues rockers Red Red Meat. The band signed to Sub Pop in 1992, only a matter of weeks after releasing their self-titled debut album, and then they went on tour with the Pumpkins. At the time, Johnson was dating bandmate Tim Rutili, but when the relationship ended, she left the band. Later in the year, Johnson sadly passed away due to complications relating to AIDS.

In October 1993, Arista Records released the *No Alternative* compilation to benefit AIDS relief, the album featuring a host of alt rock bands such as Soundgarden, Nirvana, Soul Asylum, and, of course, The Smashing Pumpkins. Looking back on contributing to the album, Billy Corgan spoke of the negativity surrounding Johnson's death at the time, when there was still a stigma surrounding the AIDS disease:

> There were things written about her and there's a lot of people who knew her better than I. But it really affected me because, not so much – and I don't want to undermine one person's passing – but it affected me more the way people talked about her dying, and the way people moralised about it, than it did the fact a human being's life had passed.

Containing mournful guitars and bass but still housing some glistening melodies, as well as what sounds like a sitar at one point as well as the harmonica, 'Glynis' captures the early '90s alt rock scene in a nutshell while also acting as a heartfelt devotion to its subject. A wailing guitar solo comes courtesy of double-tracked guitars being fed through a vintage Electro-Harmonix Bassballs pedal, leading a late charge on a song many considered to be the album's standout song.

'Dancing in the Moonlight' (Phil Lynott)

Another cover where this time the Pumpkins take on the lead single from Thin Lizzy's 1977 album, *Bad Reputation*. 'Dancing in the Moonlight' was a B-side on the Heart-covered 'Disarm' single and is slower and acoustic compared to the much more upbeat original.

It is still a nice cover that pays homage to one of the finest songwriters in rock history, the one and only Phil Lynott.

'Rudolph the Red-Nosed Reindeer' (Johnny Marks)

Recorded live at the KROQ Christmas Festival, held at the Universal Amphitheatre in Los Angeles in late 1993, Billy and his acoustic guitar covers one of the most famous Christmas songs there has ever been.

'Rudolph...' was included on the Kevin & Bean compilation, *No Toys for O.J.* in 1994, where proceeds from album sales went to the Starlight Foundation of Southern California. A non-profit organisation helping to better the lives of seriously ill children, other artists contributing Christmas covers for a worthy cause included Bad Religion, Violent Femmes, Ween and Cindy Crawford.

'Sad Peter Pan' (Vic Chestnutt)

Vic Chestnutt is a well-respected American singer/songwriter who, in 1983, was involved in a car accident which left him partially paralysed. To his credit, he went on to maintain a successful music career and earned a commercial breakthrough in 1996 upon the release of the charity record *Sweet Relief II: Gravity of the Situation*. Raising money for artists facing expensive medical bills and with no insurance, artists including the Pumpkins, R.E.M. and Garbage covered some of Chestnutt's songs.

For 'Sad Peter Pan', Red Red Meat joined the Pumpkins on a psychedelic slow burner containing a Corgan and Tim Rutili vocal duet. A nice and reflective song based around some wiry but atmospheric guitars, the song very much has the feel of The Velvet Underground, and that isn't a bad thing.

'Never Let Me Down Again' (Martin Gore)

At the request of D'arcy, who was a huge Depeche Mode fan, the Pumpkins covered one of the new wave icons' most popular songs in 1993, recording their stunning take during a visit to the *BBC* in the UK. Long before Billy Corgan would become embroiled in electronic experimentation, 'Never Let Me Down Again' is given the alt rock treatment with elevated guitar, bouncing bass and some pristine snare drumming. A B-side on the 'Rocket' single, this brilliant Pumpkins cover was given a greater platform when in 1998, the song opened the Depeche Mode tribute album, *For the Masses*.

'Czarina' (Corgan)

Assumed to have been written by Billy as an ode to girlfriend Yelena Yemchuk, whose eastern European background ties into the song title (Empresses of Russia were once known as Czarinas), the first of two B-sides on the 'Ava Adore' single is a soft and semi-acoustic love poem which Corgan is happy to share with the world. This tender passage would likely have made Yemchuk blush if nothing else-

I don't want for anything that I don't have,
All I want is waiting for me there, for me there,

With my czarina, queen of all that I believe,
Stillborn seasons cradle our affairs.

'Once in a While' (Corgan)

Containing one of the most exquisite piano pieces of any Pumpkins song, past or present, 'Once in a While' is another brilliant B-side where Corgan's soft but strained vocal evokes the emotion of every single lyric ('You'll try to care once in a while for me, and I will be there once in a while, more than a while for you.' This moving song was on the Japanese edition of *Adore*, and it made the album all the better for being included.

'Summer' (Iha)

The sole B-side on the 'Perfect' single, 'Summer', was penned by James Iha and runs the same lines as most of his previous works – slow, acoustic-orientated and exploring the theme of love. A pleasant but straightforward track that was never likely to find its way onto *Adore*, 'Summer' is another nice entry in Iha's whole-hearted discography.

Thank you for reading.

Setlist from the Pumpkins' Farewell Show at the Metro (02/12/2000)

Set One
Mellon Collie and the Infinite Sadness (Intro), Rocket, I Am One, Rhinoceros, Shame, Porcelina of the Vast Oceans, The Everlasting Gaze, Bullet with Butterfly Wings, Thru the Eyes of Ruby, Blissed and Gone, To Sheila, Mayonaise, I of the Mourning

Set Two (Acoustic)
Muzzle, Stand Inside Your Love, Perfect, This Time, Go, The Last Song, Last Instrumental, Age of Innocence, Thirty-Three

Set Three
Tonight, Tonight, Siva, Fuck You (An Ode to No One), Drown, Starla, If There Is a God, Cash Car Star, Heavy Metal Machine, Today

Encore One
For Martha, Born Under a Bad Sign (Albert King)

Encore Two
Cherub Rock

Encore Three (Acoustic)
Disarm, 1979

Encore Four
Silverfuck (lasting over 30 minutes)

Bibliography

Allmusic.com
Billboard.com
Faroutmagazine.co.uk
Genius.com
Guitarworld.com
Kerrang.com
Loudersound.com
Mtv.com
Nme.com
Pitchfork.com
Rollingstone.com
Songfacts.com
Spcodex.wiki
Spfc.org
Spin.com

Faith No More in the 90s
Decades

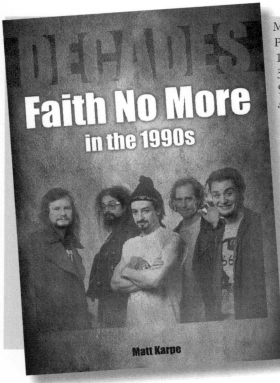

Matt Karpe
Paperback
128 pages
38 colour photographs
978-1-78951-250-1
£15.99
$22.95

The formative decade in the career of this hugely successful rock band.

It may have taken them a few years to achieve a stable line-up, but Faith No More did just that with the arrival of enigmatic frontman Mike Patton in 1988. By 1990, the San Francisco quintet were flying high on the back of their third album, *The Real Thing*, and the influential anthem for a generation, 'Epic'. Becoming a household name and mainstream chart botherers with colourful and diverse songs ranging in style from heavy metal to jazz, and rap rock to lounge music, Faith No More refused to follow trends and instead pushed forward with a gung-ho attitude and a talent for songwriting built around sonic experimentation.

The band released the critically acclaimed *Angel Dust*, as well as *King for a Day...Fool for a Lifetime* and the ironically titled *Album of the Year*, before stunning fans by parting ways in 1998. *Faith No More in the 1990s* is the story of a largely rewarding but tension-filled decade for rock music's greatest underdogs.

Providing a detailed timeline of events, frenetic touring schedules, and, most importantly, the songs, this book documents the rise and progression of one of the most distinctive bands of all time.

Tool - *on track*
every album, every song

Matt Karpe
Paperback
128 pages
33 colour photographs
978-1-78951-234-1
£15.99
$22.95

**Every album and
every song by these
rock legends.**

Music may not have been the designated career path for the members of Tool when they each relocated to Los Angeles in the 1980s, but the quartet would soon find one another and join forces to become one of the most distinctive acts in the history of rock and metal. *Tool On Track* documents all of the band's studio releases, from their raw and unapologetic 1991 demo tape to their 2019 epic, *Fear Inoculum*, a record thirteen years in the making and an album that would solidify Tool as one of the greatest progressive rock bands of all time.

Something of an enigma but an extremely complex and intelligent band, this book goes into considerable depth as it uncovers the stories behind Tool's engrossing back catalogue. The formulations of pivotal songs such as 'Sober', 'Ænema', Schism', 'Lateralus' and 'Rosetta Stoned' have become stories of legend, and this book has been extensively researched in order to create a valuable reference book that all Tool fans can delve into at their leisure,

Also focusing on the band members' various side-projects and selected guest appearances, as well as acting as a detailed biography, this is the most comprehensive book on the band yet written.

Also available from Sonicbond

On Track series
Allman Brothers Band – Andrew Wild 978-1-78952-252-5
Tori Amos – Lisa Torem 978-1-78952-142-9
Aphex Twin – Beau Waddell 978-1-78952-267-9
Asia – Peter Braidis 978-1-78952-099-6
Badfinger – Robert Day-Webb 978-1-878952-176-4
Barclay James Harvest – Keith and Monica Domone 978-1-78952-067-5
Beck – Arthur Lizie 978-1-78952-258-7
The Beatles – Andrew Wild 978-1-78952-009-5
The Beatles Solo 1969-1980 – Andrew Wild 978-1-78952-030-9
Blue Oyster Cult – Jacob Holm-Lupo 978-1-78952-007-1
Blur – Matt Bishop 978-178952-164-1
Marc Bolan and T.Rex – Peter Gallagher 978-1-78952-124-5
Kate Bush – Bill Thomas 978-1-78952-097-2
Camel – Hamish Kuzminski 978-1-78952-040-8
Captain Beefheart – Opher Goodwin 978-1-78952-235-8
Caravan – Andy Boot 978-1-78952-127-6
Cardiacs – Eric Benac 978-1-78952-131-3
Nick Cave and The Bad Seeds – Dominic Sanderson 978-1-78952-240-2
Eric Clapton Solo – Andrew Wild 978-1-78952-141-2
The Clash – Nick Assirati 978-1-78952-077-4
Elvis Costello and The Attractions – Georg Purvis 978-1-78952-129-0
Crosby, Stills and Nash – Andrew Wild 978-1-78952-039-2
Creedence Clearwater Revival – Tony Thompson 978-178952-237-2
The Damned – Morgan Brown 978-1-78952-136-8
Deep Purple and Rainbow 1968-79 – Steve Pilkington 978-1-78952-002-6
Dire Straits – Andrew Wild 978-1-78952-044-6
The Doors – Tony Thompson 978-1-78952-137-5
Dream Theater – Jordan Blum 978-1-78952-050-7
Eagles – John Van der Kiste 978-1-78952-260-0
Earth, Wind and Fire – Bud Wilkins 978-1-78952-272-3
Electric Light Orchestra – Barry Delve 978-1-78952-152-8
Emerson Lake and Palmer – Mike Goode 978-1-78952-000-2
Fairport Convention – Kevan Furbank 978-1-78952-051-4
Peter Gabriel – Graeme Scarfe 978-1-78952-138-2
Genesis – Stuart MacFarlane 978-1-78952-005-7
Gentle Giant – Gary Steel 978-1-78952-058-3
Gong – Kevan Furbank 978-1-78952-082-8
Green Day – William E. Spevack 978-1-78952-261-7
Hall and Oates – Ian Abrahams 978-1-78952-167-2
Hawkwind – Duncan Harris 978-1-78952-052-1
Peter Hammill – Richard Rees Jones 978-1-78952-163-4
Roy Harper – Opher Goodwin 978-1-78952-130-6

Jimi Hendrix – Emma Stott 978-1-78952-175-7
The Hollies – Andrew Darlington 978-1-78952-159-7
Horslips – Richard James 978-1-78952-263-1
The Human League and The Sheffield Scene –
Andrew Darlington 978-1-78952-186-3
The Incredible String Band – Tim Moon 978-1-78952-107-8
Iron Maiden – Steve Pilkington 978-1-78952-061-3
Joe Jackson – Richard James 978-1-78952-189-4
Jefferson Airplane – Richard Butterworth 978-1-78952-143-6
Jethro Tull – Jordan Blum 978-1-78952-016-3
Elton John in the 1970s – Peter Kearns 978-1-78952-034-7
Billy Joel – Lisa Torem 978-1-78952-183-2
Judas Priest – John Tucker 978-1-78952-018-7
Kansas – Kevin Cummings 978-1-78952-057-6
The Kinks – Martin Hutchinson 978-1-78952-172-6
Korn – Matt Karpe 978-1-78952-153-5
Led Zeppelin – Steve Pilkington 978-1-78952-151-1
Level 42 – Matt Philips 978-1-78952-102-3
Little Feat – Georg Purvis - 978-1-78952-168-9
Aimee Mann – Jez Rowden 978-1-78952-036-1
Joni Mitchell – Peter Kearns 978-1-78952-081-1
The Moody Blues – Geoffrey Feakes 978-1-78952-042-2
Motorhead – Duncan Harris 978-1-78952-173-3
Nektar – Scott Meze – 978-1-78952-257-0
New Order – Dennis Remmer – 978-1-78952-249-5
Nightwish – Simon McMurdo – 978-1-78952-270-9
Laura Nyro – Philip Ward 978-1-78952-182-5
Mike Oldfield – Ryan Yard 978-1-78952-060-6
Opeth – Jordan Blum 978-1-78-952-166-5
Pearl Jam – Ben L. Connor 978-1-78952-188-7
Tom Petty – Richard James 978-1-78952-128-3
Pink Floyd – Richard Butterworth 978-1-78952-242-6
The Police – Pete Braidis 978-1-78952-158-0
Porcupine Tree – Nick Holmes 978-1-78952-144-3
Queen – Andrew Wild 978-1-78952-003-3
Radiohead – William Allen 978-1-78952-149-8
Rancid – Paul Matts 989-1-78952-187-0
Renaissance – David Detmer 978-1-78952-062-0
REO Speedwagon – Jim Romag 978-1-78952-262-4
The Rolling Stones 1963-80 – Steve Pilkington 978-1-78952-017-0
The Smiths and Morrissey – Tommy Gunnarsson 978-1-78952-140-5
Spirit – Rev. Keith A. Gordon – 978-1-78952- 248-8
Stackridge – Alan Draper 978-1-78952-232-7

Status Quo the Frantic Four Years – Richard James 978-1-78952-160-3
Steely Dan – Jez Rowden 978-1-78952-043-9
Steve Hackett – Geoffrey Feakes 978-1-78952-098-9
Tears For Fears – Paul Clark - 978-178952-238-9
Thin Lizzy – Graeme Stroud 978-1-78952-064-4
Tool – Matt Karpe 978-1-78952-234-1
Toto – Jacob Holm-Lupo 978-1-78952-019-4
U2 – Eoghan Lyng 978-1-78952-078-1
UFO – Richard James 978-1-78952-073-6
Van Der Graaf Generator – Dan Coffey 978-1-78952-031-6
Van Halen – Morgan Brown – 9781-78952-256-3
The Who – Geoffrey Feakes 978-1-78952-076-7
Roy Wood and the Move – James R Turner 978-1-78952-008-8
Yes – Stephen Lambe 978-1-78952-001-9
Frank Zappa 1966 to 1979 – Eric Benac 978-1-78952-033-0
Warren Zevon – Peter Gallagher 978-1-78952-170-2
10CC – Peter Kearns 978-1-78952-054-5

Decades Series

The Bee Gees in the 1960s – Andrew Mon Hughes et al 978-1-78952-148-1
The Bee Gees in the 1970s – Andrew Mon Hughes et al 978-1-78952-179-5
Black Sabbath in the 1970s – Chris Sutton 978-1-78952-171-9
Britpop – Peter Richard Adams and Matt Pooler 978-1-78952-169-6
Phil Collins in the 1980s – Andrew Wild 978-1-78952-185-6
Alice Cooper in the 1970s – Chris Sutton 978-1-78952-104-7
Alice Cooper in the 1980s – Chris Sutton 978-1-78952-259-4
Curved Air in the 1970s – Laura Shenton 978-1-78952-069-9
Donovan in the 1960s – Jeff Fitzgerald 978-1-78952-233-4
Bob Dylan in the 1980s – Don Klees 978-1-78952-157-3
Brian Eno in the 1970s – Gary Parsons 978-1-78952-239-6
Faith No More in the 1990s – Matt Karpe 978-1-78952-250-1
Fleetwood Mac in the 1970s – Andrew Wild 978-1-78952-105-4
Fleetwood Mac in the 1980s – Don Klees 978-178952-254-9
Focus in the 1970s – Stephen Lambe 978-1-78952-079-8
Free and Bad Company in the 1970s – John Van der Kiste 978-1-78952-178-8
Genesis in the 1970s – Bill Thomas 978178952-146-7
George Harrison in the 1970s – Eoghan Lyng 978-1-78952-174-0
Kiss in the 1970s – Peter Gallagher 978-1-78952-246-4
Manfred Mann's Earth Band in the 1970s – John Van der Kiste 978178952-243-3
Marillion in the 1980s – Nathaniel Webb 978-1-78952-065-1
Van Morrison in the 1970s – Peter Childs - 978-1-78952-241-9
Mott the Hoople and Ian Hunter in the 1970s –
John Van der Kiste 978-1-78-952-162-7

Pink Floyd In The 1970s – Georg Purvis 978-1-78952-072-9
Suzi Quatro in the 1970s – Darren Johnson 978-1-78952-236-5
Queen in the 1970s – James Griffiths 978-1-78952-265-5
Roxy Music in the 1970s – Dave Thompson 978-1-78952-180-1
Slade in the 1970s – Darren Johnson 978-1-78952-268-6
Status Quo in the 1980s – Greg Harper 978-1-78952-244-0
Tangerine Dream in the 1970s – Stephen Palmer 978-1-78952-161-0
The Sweet in the 1970s – Darren Johnson 978-1-78952-139-9
Uriah Heep in the 1970s – Steve Pilkington 978-1-78952-103-0
Van der Graaf Generator in the 1970s – Steve Pilkington 978-1-78952-245-7
Rick Wakeman in the 1970s – Geoffrey Feakes 978-1-78952-264-8
Yes in the 1980s – Stephen Lambe with David Watkinson 978-1-78952-125-2

On Screen series
Carry On... – Stephen Lambe 978-1-78952-004-0
David Cronenberg – Patrick Chapman 978-1-78952-071-2
Doctor Who: The David Tennant Years – Jamie Hailstone 978-1-78952-066-8
James Bond – Andrew Wild 978-1-78952-010-1
Monty Python – Steve Pilkington 978-1-78952-047-7
Seinfeld Seasons 1 to 5 – Stephen Lambe 978-1-78952-012-5

Other Books
1967: A Year In Psychedelic Rock 978-1-78952-155-9
1970: A Year In Rock – John Van der Kiste 978-1-78952-147-4
1973: The Golden Year of Progressive Rock 978-1-78952-165-8
Babysitting A Band On The Rocks – G.D. Praetorius 978-1-78952-106-1
Eric Clapton Sessions – Andrew Wild 978-1-78952-177-1
Derek Taylor: For Your Radioactive Children –
Andrew Darlington 978-1-78952-038-5
The Golden Road: The Recording History of The Grateful Dead – John Kilbride 978-1-78952-156-6
Iggy and The Stooges On Stage 1967-1974 – Per Nilsen 978-1-78952-101-6
Jon Anderson and the Warriors – the road to Yes –
David Watkinson 978-1-78952-059-0
Magic: The David Paton Story – David Paton 978-1-78952-266-2
Misty: The Music of Johnny Mathis – Jakob Baekgaard 978-1-78952-247-1
Nu Metal: A Definitive Guide – Matt Karpe 978-1-78952-063-7
Tommy Bolin: In and Out of Deep Purple – Laura Shenton 978-1-78952-070-5
Maximum Darkness – Deke Leonard 978-1-78952-048-4
The Twang Dynasty – Deke Leonard 978-1-78952-049-1

and many more to come!

Would you like to write for Sonicbond Publishing?

At Sonicbond Publishing we are always on the look-out for authors, particularly for our two main series:

On Track. Mixing fact with in depth analysis, the On Track series examines the work of a particular musical artist or group. All genres are considered from easy listening and jazz to 60s soul to 90s pop, via rock and metal.

On Screen. This series looks at the world of film and television. Subjects considered include directors, actors and writers, as well as entire television and film series. As with the On Track series, we balance fact with analysis.

While professional writing experience would, of course, be an advantage the most important qualification is to have real enthusiasm and knowledge of your subject. First-time authors are welcomed, but the ability to write well in English is essential.

Sonicbond Publishing has distribution throughout Europe and North America, and all books are also published in E-book form. Authors will be paid a royalty based on sales of their book.

Further details are available from www.sonicbondpublishing.co.uk. To contact us, complete the contact form there or
email info@sonicbondpublishing.co.uk